Preparing
Learners for
e-Learning

George M. Piskurich
Editor

Pfeiffer
A Wiley Imprint
www.pfeiffer.com

Published by Pfeiffer
An Imprint of Wiley
989 Market Street, San Francisco, CA 94103-1741   www.pfeiffer.com

Pfeiffer books and products are available through most bookstores. To contact Pfeiffer directly, call our Customer Care Department within the U.S. at (800) 274-4434, outside the U.S. at (317) 572-3985 or fax (317) 572-4002.

Pfeiffer also publishes its books in a variety of electronic formats. Some content that appears in print may not be available in electronic books.
ISBN: 0-7879-6396-8

Library of Congress Cataloging-in-Publication Data

Piskurich, George M.
    Preparing learners for e-Learning / George M. Piskurich.
      p. cm.
    Includes bibliographical references and index.
    ISBN 0-7879-6396-8
    1. Employees—Training of. I. Title.
HF5549.5.T7 P545 2003
658.3'124'02854369—dc21

                           2002152165

Acquiring Editor: Matthew Davis
Director of Development: Kathleen Dolan Davies
Editor: Rebecca Taff
Senior Production Editor: Dawn Kilgore
Manufacturing Supervisor: Bill Matherly
Cover Design: Chris Wallace

Contents

List of
Figures and Tables

Chapter 4

Chapter 5

Chapter 6

Chapter 7

Chapter 8

Chapter 10

Introduction

E-LEARNERS FAIL! Not one or two, here and there, but large numbers of them. Some studies suggest more than half of would-be e-learners either never take advantage of e-learning possibilities or never finish their first program. There are a lot of reasons for this statistic—poor course design, poor motivation, lack of applicability, barriers erected in their way—but often the failure is due to the fact that the learners were simply not prepared to become e-learners.

Most learners find e-learning to be a very different and often unsettling experience. It does not provide them with the sense of comfort and security they find in the classroom, where the instructor tells you what you need to know and expects you to be back in your seat on time. From long experience, they understand the classroom and what is expected of them there. They are not as sure of their role in e-learning.

Preparing learners to be self-directed enough to be comfortable with e-learning and to use it effectively is critical to their success in the process. As learner drop-out or non-compliance is one of the key factors in the failure of many e-learning interventions, the information presented here on this and other related topics is relevant to anyone who is responsible for making e-learning happen.

PURPOSE

The purpose of this book is to present a variety of ways by which both business organizations and educational institutions can prepare learners to succeed at e-learning. Its major thrust is in the process of augmenting the learners' self-directedness so that they can take full advantage of e-learning initiatives, which are basically self-directed learning processes. However, there is also plenty of information on the mechanics of what an organization needs to do to prepare and support the self-directed e-learner.

Both of these aspects are as relevant for a business about to embark on an e-learning initiative as for an academic environment in which new students need to enhance their self-directedness before they can effectively utilize e-learning classes.

AUDIENCE

Our intended audience for this book is those who create and deliver e-learning in the business sector and their managers, as well as distance learning professors and administrators in public education.

A secondary audience is the e-learners themselves, who can use this book as a guide for their own individual preparation to becoming more efficient at e-learning

SCOPE AND TREATMENT

While the information presented here is not new to the small cadre of individuals who have been studying self-direction for many years, it is probably very new to the majority of practitioners who have not realized that there is a need to help learners psychologically and physically prepare for e-learning. Much of the research and practical information you will find here will be unique, and we hope eye-opening for you.

Each chapter has been written by an expert in learner preparation, some from the academic community, others from the business world, and many who span both environments as professors and consultants. We've asked each of our authors to use his or her own unique perspective in writing and did not hamstring them with a particular format or chapter plan.

This has created a rather eclectic mix of educational research and practical application among the chapters, ranging from discussions of self-directed learning theory to descriptions of specific learner preparation mechanisms that have proven effective in various environments.

By looking at the process from a number of different perspectives, we feel this book relates to all levels and environments of those who create and manage e-learning.

CONTENT SUMMARY

While the chapters have differences in structure and language, they all have the same goal—to help you prepare your learners to become effective and confident e-learners.

In the first chapter, Doctor Huey Long, one of the founding fathers of self-directed learning theory, sets our stage with a discussion of self-direction as a prerequisite to e-learning. He provides a look at why people are not self-directed enough to take full advantage of e-learning and gives us a list of ways we can help enhance our learners' self-directedness.

Paul and Lucy Guglielmino expand on Long's foundation with information on how to identify learners who are ready for e-learning and how to support them. They discuss the components of e-learner readiness and relate them to the self-directed learner's attitudes and abilities. They finish up with a discussion of the Self-Directed Learning Readiness Scale, an instrument that can be used to determine learner readiness to engage in self-directed activities such as e-learning

Richard Durr is next, discussing learner preparation for e-learning from the point of view of one who has been there. He discusses Motorola's experiences in providing e-learning to its thousands of employees, with particular emphasis on the use of learners' guides to help support and orient the new e-learner.

George and Janet Piskurich continue Richard Durr's theme with a look at a specific mechanism for enhancing self-directedness in e-learners, using, strangely enough, a classroom. They provide us with an actual outline for how to produce a face-to-face process that combines both developmental and organizational activities into a system that enhances self-direction in employees who are about to embark on e-learning.

Rick Rabideau's perspective is that of a learning manager as he gives us insights on e-learning and the various techniques he used to prepare both his company and his e-learners for a switch from classroom-based instruction to e-learning.

Jim Moshinski (better known as "Doctor Mo") encompasses both the academic and business worlds with his report on best practices for preparing the learner and the organization for a better e-learning experience. These ideas were collected from "e-LITE" (e-Learning Incites Training Excellence), a weekly web-based training think tank devoted to discussing e-learning issues. His tips run the gamut from building stakeholder support to assessing metacognitive strategies.

Ronnie Kurchner-Hawkins continues our discussion of the organizational aspects of learner preparation in her chapter, giving us some great insights into what's actually happening to the organization when we try to initiate e-learning, with a case-study-based commentary using the diffusion of innovation model. She provides us with a list of adopter characteristics that are critical to successful e-learners.

In Chapter 8 George Siemens and Stephen Yurkiw provide an academic perspective by relating their experiences in developing an e-learning initiative in a university setting. They discuss the similarities and differences of e-learning to classroom learning and e-learners to classroom learners, then look at the role of the organization, the learner, and the instructor in creating e-learning success.

Paul Carr and Michael Ponton continue our look at the synchronous e-learning instructor's role in preparing and supporting the e-learner with a discussion of building collegial relationships over the e-learning process as an important aspect in enhancing self-direction in e-learners. They give us a complete background of the research involved in this process, as well as its possible results.

Terry Redding adds one more perspective to our mix by discussing the preparation of e-learners from the e-learning vendor's point of view. He discusses methods for screening and orienting e-learners, as well as ways to remove barriers and provide initial and ongoing support, and the use of course validation as a preparation factor.

The last chapter is a bit different. It is a compilation of quotes on e-learning from those who matter most, the e-learners. If you want to know what "they" really think, this might be the place to find out.

HOW TO USE THIS BOOK

As you might expect, the most effective way to use this book is any way that suits your situation best. Read it cover to cover or skip around the chapters looking for knowledge to meet your immediate needs. It has been created to give you a number of perspectives on the same general topic, but those perspectives can vary greatly. We hope this brief introduction will help guide you toward where you need to go to get the answers and ideas that will allow you to successfully prepare your learners for e-learning.

Chapter 1

Preparing e-Learners for Self-Directed Learning

Huey B. Long

Comments from e-Learners

"I can't learn what nobody teaches me."

"I'm not motivated."

HOW CAN E-LEARNERS BE PREPARED for self-directed learning, which is a term for directing and managing their own learning? Implicit in the question is the assumption that there is someone or something that can prepare e-learners to take greater responsibility for their learning. The question is important because of monumental technological advances in the areas of information management and communication that have the potential for drastically altering the learning landscape. Many believe that learners' activity will be changed in dramatic ways in the near future. One scenario that casts learners in a more independent role is reflected in discussions of self-directed learning (Long, 2001). But there are a few difficulties in the transition to self-directed learning based on e-learning, as some adults may prefer traditional instructional formats. To further complicate the task, some adults may not be attracted to e-learning media. Why might this be true? What or who can help prepare adults for a self-directed learning activity?

This chapter addresses the key question raised in the above paragraph. There is a simple answer to the question, but the answer raises additional questions that are more difficult to resolve. See the conclusion for the simple answer!

We assume that the e-learners with whom we are concerned are not participating under duress and are voluntarily addressing learning goals. Here, e-learners, that is, individuals who are pursuing their learning goals through the use of electronic modes, fall into one of two groups: (1) autodidactic learners who personally plan and conduct all of the tasks and activities associated with their learning; and (2) individuals who engage in learning as a part of some kind of group with some kind of shared aspect of the learning goals (objectives and purposes, materials, activities, sources of information, application, and evaluation and assessment). The first kind of e-learner is assumed to have already become a self-directed learner, and as such is already prepared for that role. Therefore, we are primarily interested in the second kind of e-learner—the person who is engaged in learning as part of a group, or one who is expected to initiate an e-learning activity. In the former scenario, it is assumed there is a group leader, referred to as a facilitator, who has content or skill expertise. The facilitator has prepared in advance to lead the group in the e-learning activity using a design and techniques based on self-directed learning, such as learner choice, personal learner control, selection, input and negotiations concerning goals, activities, application, product, and evaluation. The latter scenario is less clear, as it may include the novice e-learner who has received encouragement from some authority to plug in for some kind of online learning activity, purchase a software program, or "surf the web." In the first situation there is usually someone from whom the learner may obtain encouragement, assistance, and guidance. In the latter, all such assistance, if available, may be electronic and impersonal. While these two scenarios are quite different, the self-directed e-learners in each situation may have some similar needs.

Unfortunately, before the potential of self-directed learning in e-learning can be reached, a number of significant problems must be resolved. Before discussing and illustrating ways that e-learners may be prepared for self-direction, it is desirable to ask why any learner engaged in any kind of learning activity might need to be prepared for self-directed learning. Therefore, this chapter is divided into two major divisions. The first section deals with the problem in two subsections: *conceptual difficulties* and *obstacles*. The second section focuses on a *strategy* to facilitate the preparation of learners for self-directed learning.

THE PROBLEM

Self-direction in e-learning is fundamentally similar to self-direction in other formats and modes. Self-direction in learning is enhanced by a variety of phenomena: learner psychological characteristics such as perseverance, ability to manage adversity, motivation, competence in setting goals, reasoning, memory, cognitive regulation, and so forth. Long (2000) identifies three primary dimensions of self-direction in learning:

- Motivation
- Metacognition
- Self-regulation

The above are supported by four secondary dimensions: *choice, competence, control,* and *confidence*. Modality and media comprise the greatest difference between self-directed learners using e-learning modes and learners who traditionally have been dependent on written materials and personal observations. Before there was e-learning, there was correspondence study, learning by observation, coaching, on-the-job training, and classroom learning. Self-directed learning was possible in all of the above, and self-directed learning activities in each of the above were affected in some way by the environment and modality. It was possible for an individual learning via one of the above modes to engage in other-directed learning also. Therefore, e-learning itself does not guarantee self-direction and self-directed learning does not require the electronic mode.

Conceptual Difficulties

Self-management and direction of learning by adults and children are referred to often as self-direction in learning, self-directed learning, and self-regulated learning. The adjectives in the above terms focus attention on the control of learning by the learner, rather than control by an external force. Self-responsibility is fundamental to self-directed learning in e-learning or any other kind of learning.

Learner acceptance of personal responsibility in learning is often limited by two major social conditions. Space does not permit a full explication of these conditions here, but it is sufficient to briefly note that since about 1850–1875, as teaching and schooling became a central part of a child's culture in the United States, the learner's role in learning has been neglected in favor of teachers' professional teaching activities. Unfortunately, the idea that learners have an active responsibility in learning has received much less attention in the literature than has teacher responsibility. In a way these developments mirror the four C's of self-directed learning: teacher *choice*, teacher *control*, teacher determination of *competence*, and teacher attribution of *confidence*.

The relative neglect of the learner's role in learning is accompanied by actions that inhibit the use of self-directed learning activities and learner expectations. Learners are developed from childhood to expect learning to occur in formal situations, under the strict guidance of a teacher. Thus, even though most individuals are competent managers of much of their learning (Ravid, 1986), often without the assistance of trainers and teachers, learner acceptance of the responsibility for learning is problematic in certain settings. Paradoxically, while adults usually prefer freedom and independence of action, they often expect the control and supervision of trainers and teachers in formal training and education settings. This expectation appears to contribute to discomfort when the control is minimal or absent. As a result, expectations of teacher/trainer control are usually present in adult teaching/training, even though adults have had a variety of successful learning experiences that were free of a formal teacher's effort. This expectation seems to prevail, even though studies indicate that approximately 80 percent of what managers and professionals learn occurs as a result of learner self-direction (Graeve, 1987; Straka, Klienmann, & Stokl, 1994). That is, most of what they learn takes place beyond formal training or instructional environments.

Trainers and educators are aware of the threat raised by mentioning and expecting their trainees and students to be self-directed learners, so they, too, often avoid designing programs based on self-direction. Or they attempt to slip the self-directed aspects into the program surreptitiously. The scheme discussed in this chapter is designed to overtly and covertly introduce self-direction in ways that help the learner avoid the psychological threat. Use of the procedures suggested in the following pages will reinforce the adult's natural tendency to be self-directing and independent, while helping the learners come to grips with the reality of their own ability to be self-directed.

Obstacles to Self-Directed Learning

Before introducing trainees and students to self-directed learning in any kind of formal learning situation (including e-learning schemes), we need to be aware of some of the obstacles learners face. Three important barriers to acceptance of personal responsibility in learning are as follows: (1) the learners' previous formal training and instruction have provided limited opportunity for learner responsibility in those settings; (2) past experiences with self-direction in formal settings have been negative; and (3) failure to relate learning goals to learners' personal interests.

Efforts to prepare learners to be self-directed should consider how the above are obstacles to adoption of self-directed learning. In either direct or indirect ways, learners should be provided the opportunity to face the possibility of simultaneously holding two different concepts of learner responsibility: dependent learning based on teacher dominance and learner centered self-directed learning. Facilitators should review their teaching plans to foster depth processing and productive learning and reduce surface processing and reproductive learning. In other words, teachers and trainers should improve and increase their efforts to address application, interpretation, and understanding, while reducing emphasis on recall and memorization. Finally, some method should be devised to enable learners to increase their personal stake and interest in the topic.

PREPARING LEARNERS FOR SELF-DIRECTION

If it is true that 80 percent of the learning of managers and professionals is accomplished in a self-directed mode, why do we need to prepare learners to be self-directed learners? Stated another way, the question becomes a paradoxical statement as follows: Even though managers and professionals are adept at self-directing learning, they seem to be reluctant to engage in such learning in formal education and training settings. A follow-up question is: Is there any reason to believe they will be more likely to be self-directing in the use of e-learning? Whether the situation is presented as a question or as a statement, it is apparent that we have a problem. If, as already noted, there are some obstacles to self-directed learning, are there any measures that we can take to overcome the negative forces?

The following discussion is based on certain assumptions that are important. As noted in the second paragraph of this chapter, the answer to how to prepare e-learners to be self-directed learners is a simple one. Positive experience with being a self-directed learner is the answer. Such experience is gained in two ways: One is serendipitous, and the other is intentional. By the former means, the learner discovers within himself or herself the drive to be self-directed as a result of personality and circumstances. By the latter means, someone or something places the learner in a situation where self-directed learning occurs more by design than by choice of the learner. In either way, however, the learner discovers that he or she is capable of being a self-directed learner. Naturally, we would not endeavor to outline a lifestyle that would provide the serendipitous experience. Therefore, we are assuming that we have a responsible party, a trainer, an administrator, or a teacher of some kind, who seeks to strengthen self-directed learning within individuals for whom he or she has some responsibility. It is further assumed that the above individual will devise some kind of lesson(s) to be delivered by electronic or human means. The above assumptions, therefore, do not address the autodidactic.

A variety of procedures are available to the trainer and teacher that help prepare individuals for self-directed learning. For our purposes here, we propose that there are general learner variables (classed as state and trait phenomena) that may either encourage or discourage a learner's participation in self-directed learning. For example, momentary fear of the unknown aspects of self-directed learning is a state condition, as is excited expectation. A persistent lifelong fear or anxiety, however, is a trait. The momentary fear should be easier to overcome by encouragement than the lifelong kind is. A dependent personality is a trait, as is an inner-controlled one. The discussion of trait and state phenomena is not intended to complicate the problem; instead they are mentioned to identify the difficulties in preparing someone to be self-directed. In order to encourage self-directed learning, both state and trait variables need to be addressed. Awareness of the problem is useful in devising a strategy for preparing learners for self-direction if learning is desirable. For purposes of convenience, the strategy may include procedures that can be described as being of two types: direct and indirect. Until the trainer-educator learns how to use both types of procedures in a normal and automatic manner, every training and instructional design should make the procedures discussed in the following pages explicit.

Strategies for Preparing for Self-Directed Learning

The foregoing discussion provides a framework for the development of a strategy for encouraging self-directed learning. The over-arching goal is to design a situation where the learner has some success with self-directed learning. In addition to the following examples, the reader may wish to refer to Grow (1991) and Piskurich (2001). Grow proposes that learners may progressively move from a dependent state to a self-directed state with the assistance of facilitators. Piskurich describes a process that may be used in the early stages of the learning activity that is similar to the procedures discussed in this chapter. The strategy adopted will influence the procedures. It is convenient to think of strategy being either *direct* or *indirect*. A strategy of direct action will employ procedures that overtly communicate and sustain the learning activities. In contrast, an indirect strategy leads to more covert activities, and learners may not readily identify them as a form of self-direction. The differences between the two strategies should be obvious as the discussion unfolds.

Seven Principles

Regardless of the strategy adopted, there are some common principles. These are closely related to the three primary dimensions and four secondary dimensions following Long (2000), as mentioned above.

First, the facilitator should recognize that in many instances learners are being challenged psychologically to abandon a familiar process and its security to adopt an unknown and threatening process.

Second, as discussed in the early pages of this chapter, learners have to change their perspective to appreciate and value self-directed learning.

Third, learners have to recognize that they can successfully engage in self-directed learning in formal education and training as well as in informal learning.

Fourth, they need to be aware that effective learning does not always follow a direct path.

Fifth, learners must have a basic competence in information processing, goal development, decision-making skills, and some aptitude in the area under study.

Sixth, they need reinforcement from the facilitator to support them in the early stages of self-directed learning when they may begin to doubt themselves.

Seventh, not all learners will progress from being a highly dependent learner to being a very self-directed learner during one learning activity.

Facilitators should keep the above seven principles in mind during all of their efforts to prepare learners for self-directed learning.

Direct Strategy

Direct procedures include those activities available to the trainer and teacher to address needs that reside within the learner. Primarily, these procedures are specially designed to explicitly create learner awareness of the positive and negative variables that may affect self-direction in learning. Usually, this strategy may be more confrontational than an indirect one. Here learners are put into a position that requires them to explicitly face the prospects of being self-directed in their learning. It is suggested that the indirect procedures follow the direct procedures. For example, if the teacher/trainer strategy is a direct one, the kinds of procedures identified in the discussion of an indirect strategy are useful. In contrast, if an indirect strategy is adopted, some of the procedures identified with the direct strategy may be inappropriate.

Some direct procedures that may be followed, adhering to the seven principles discussed above, are briefly discussed below. Note that these procedures may be described as those that (1) contribute to self-awareness; (2) provide encouragement; (3) contribute to recognition of prior success; (4) create personal ownership; (5) encourage acceptance of procedures; and (6) provide learner support. A fundamental rule is: Keep the threat level to a minimum!

Establish a personal profile. The facilitator will select and use one of the available diagnostic instruments such as the Guglielmino

Self-Directed Learning Readiness Scale or some other procedure. Once the results are available, the learner engages in an introspective analysis of the results based on guidelines established for the selected scale. If help is requested, assistance in interpretation should be available. Following the identification of a learner's profile, the leaders can implement some or all of the following activities.

Use biography, fiction literature, or movie sources that illustrate self-directed learning. Biographies of Thomas Edison (Adler, 1990; Edison, 1971), Marie Curie (Quinn, 1995), Peter the Great (Massie, 1980), and Wilder Penfield (Lewis, 1981) illustrate the genre. The facilitator may ask the learner to choose one of the above based on personal interest. Then the reader will be prepared to analyze and discuss the key attributes and goals of the selected person. For example, the learner (directly or indirectly) should be able to see how both Penfield and Peter the Great made observations and made illustrations of things they wanted to remember or study. Differences between their procedures can also be examined by the learners. The drive of Thomas Edison and Marie Curie to solve problems illustrates perseverance and problem posing as well as risk taking. Be aware that different biographers emphasize different parts and activities in the life of their subject; as a result, not all biographies illustrate self-directed learning in the same way. Also, biographies may be selected based on the personal and professional backgrounds of the learners. Then there are multiple biographical studies such as Dekruif's (1926) modern classic *The Microbe Hunters* and Samuel Smile's (1866) *Self-Help*. Most of Louis L'Amour's frontier books illustrate self-direction in learning. I especially like *The Walking Drum* (L'Amour, 1985). Other examples of fiction include *Jude the Obscure* (Hardy, 1923), and *Pillars of the Earth* (Follett, 1989). Movies such as *Jonathan Livingston Seagull* and *October Skies* can be useful also. All or parts of the above can be selected for group or individual readings and discussion. Almost all of the above illustrate in some way personal drives that overcame almost insurmountable challenges. Dissatisfaction with the status quo and the need to determine why something happened or could happen characterize many of the above stories. A deep trust in one's own ability, mission, or goal is also common to most.

Remember that the purpose of using the works of artists such as the above is to exploit the sources' communicative power. They can reach emotions and develop responses that cannot be touched by other materials. Artistic treatment of the overcoming human spirit driven to achieve, master unknowns, and solve mysteries can touch depths of human understanding in special ways. They can equally represent and reinforce the meaning of the challenges and victories of the human journey for any one of us. The leader may approach the literature in at least two ways. One approach would be to provide a set of prepared questions to guide the learner through the reading material and then discuss the responses in terms of how self-directed learning is illustrated or developed. Another less directed approach is to ask the learner to search for themes in one or more readings that illustrate aspects of self-directed learning. A discussion of the themes follows, with encouragement to apply the insights to the learner's personal learning approach.

Use case studies from organizations and individuals that reinforce the positive aspects of self-directed learning. See Piskurich (2001) for additional suggestions.

Plan and conduct a meaningful discussion, at the first meeting, face-to-face or online, of examples of the learners' own self-directed learning. Ask each learner to identify something that he or she has learned in the past year. Then ask them specifically to identify how they learned it.

Move the discussion to self-directed learning projects at work and leisure. Many adults are regularly engaged in team problem solving at the workplace. They tend to overlook those activities when discussing their learning. Most leisure-related learning including hobbies is pursed in a self-directed manner. Home repairs and gardening are additional examples of self-directed learning. Encourage the group to discuss how and why they were effective in the above activities and how that might contrast/compare to formal learning.

Break the learning activity into segments related to overall tasks and goals. Engage the learners in establishing how and why the goals and content are important to them. Encourage them to select appropriate aspects of the goals that may be modified so that each learner can connect it to his or her personal interests.

Ask learners to look for and identify personally interesting or beneficial elements in the learning activity. Get them to discuss why it is important to learn what they have selected.

Be available for continuing support and encouragement. If you are seeking to move the learner into e-learning, strongly encourage the use of the computer as a means of communication.

Indirect Strategy

In contrast with the direct procedures to encourage self-directing learning discussed above, there are some more subtle and indirect procedures that may be used. These procedures may be considered covert, as they do not necessarily call attention to the self-direction qualities. I have selected nine indirect procedures in the following pages. They are (1) posing questions, (2) posing problems, (3) creating questions, (4) working with paradoxes, (5) energizing enigmas, (6) facing dilemmas, (7) supporting inquiry, (8) applying models and principles, and (9) using existing abilities and interests. Please note these are not mutually exclusive activities. An instructional design could conceivably include most, if not all, of the procedures in a course, seminar, or workshop. As with the direct procedures, the indirect procedures share some common abstract qualities. They call upon the use of learner application, challenge, curiosity, creativity, and reinforcement.

As mentioned above, if desired, these may also be used following or during the more direct procedures discussed in the previous section. The length of the schedule, or availability of time, would influence the variety of the procedures.

Posing Questions. Much of teaching and training in the traditional sense emphasizes the giving of information. Unfortunately, giving information too often leads to the end of inquiry. Self-directed learning can be encouraged by presenting questions for analysis, examination, and discussion. Questions can be cascaded to move from the simple to the complex, from the known to the unknown. For example, a recall question primarily is used to check on memory, while an analytical question may be used to examine understanding. This is illustrated as follows: What was the name of the first transcontinental railroad? What kind of economic impact did it have on the United States? What other kinds of major developments can be traced to the railroad? How important are railroads in the United States today? How do railroad freight and passenger service compare? Why? If you were to create a new rail system in the United States, what would it look like? See the differences in the questions and how they require different cognitive action!

Questions can be posed by careful advance planning and by extemporaneous response to learner comments. All questions should not be the product of the facilitator; learners are expected to pose questions in response to discussion.

Creating Questions. This procedure requires learners to devise their own questions in response to information given or in anticipation of information to emerge. For example, ask the learners to review a critical document such as an annual report, business plan, or proposal. Then encourage the learners to construct three questions that the document raised. (A similar approach may be used concerning a course syllabus.) The questions may be about something mentioned but not discussed in detail, or it may be a question about implications for the future, or a question about factual support. In other words, the questions are designed to get the learner into a thinking mode as opposed to an absorption mode. Early in the activity, learner-created questions may be accepted for examination and discussion in a nonjudgmental manner. As time progresses, however, the quality of the questions should become a topic of consideration. The learners should work to establish criteria to discriminate between frivolous questions and substantive ones.

Posing Problems. Learners may be presented with a problem by the facilitator or they may be requested to pose a problem that is resolved intellectually. For example, years ago automobile manufacturers were confronted with a discrepancy between their production of vehicles and available paint drying sheds. How could the problem best be solved? In another instance, someone identified the railroad problems with a limited view of the train and transportation business—they said management thought they were in the railroad business instead of being in the transportation industry. What kinds of problems are suggested by this observation? How can that situation be presented as a problem? Furthermore, once the problem has been posed, how may it be resolved? Competing solutions should be open for identification and resolution.

Working with Paradoxes. Paradoxes are useful attention getters. Usually a paradox is based on a discrepancy between an expected outcome (or event) and an actual one. For example, if A = B, B = C, then hypothetically A = C. But what happens when A does not equal C? How can the apparent inconsistency be explained? For example, height and weight generally are positively associated, but in some instances that association may not hold. Why? Explain. In business it is assumed that profit is associated with production, so how can one explain how profits decline after production increases? Paradoxes can be developed to reinforce a point and stimulate inquiry.

Energizing Enigmas. Enigmas present us with a mystery. For some a mystery has one purpose—and that is to be solved or at least to be addressed. Learners presented with enigmas usually cannot walk away without at least considering them. Enigmas attract attention, which usually is the first step in inquiry. For example, the world of business is filled with stories of missed opportunities; how can these missed opportunities be explained? What can be learned from them? A further example is found in business where a company undertakes a training program to solve a reporting problem in the company. But after the training the old problem remains. As a result the consultant's training program is quickly identified as the problem. But there is another, better explanation resting in the company itself. What could it be?

Facing Dilemmas. Dilemmas are not unknown in life. Most adult learners are aware of the power of dilemmas to force difficult decisions. Learners, however, may need some practice in establishing the criteria of meaningful dilemmas and superficial conflict. Facilitators may need to review their content carefully to derive appropriate dilemmas from key sources. For example, e-learning is touted as an inexpensive way to reduce current education and training, but in fictitious company X, production and labor costs increased after introducing new e-learning schemes. Some managers relate these costs to e-learning. How can this dilemma be addressed?

Supporting Inquiry. Inquiry is substantially different from instruction and can be an important way to encourage learners to become more self-directing without ever mentioning the term. William Heard Kilpatrick was noted for his attention to the development of an approach to teaching/learning that he called student's learning projects. The idea was a progression from John Dewey's emphasis on problem solving. In project learning, learners begin the inquiry with a question or problem that they intend to resolve (see above discussion about problem posing). Inquiry problems may emerge from a variety of sources, including the learners' personal interests. All learners have not learned how to develop a problem for inquiry or resolution, however. Some individual guidance may be needed to help learners transform their interest into a manageable learning problem. Problem development is often a process of thoughtful and deliberate refinement that requires time.

Applying Models and Principles. Implementation of this procedure includes any one or all of the following: identification and selection of a model from the literature or creation of a model by the group or an individual. For example, a chemistry class may use models of elements to explain the creation of a compound. Or a health provider may use existing models of human anatomy to suggest intervention alternatives. A corporation may study a business model from a different business sector. The point of using models, either existing or learner-created ones, is that learners have the opportunity to engage in theoretical thinking, inquiry, and a variety of problem-solving activities. In some topics such as human learning, a variety of models may exist and the learner has to develop a different one or critique one or more of the published models. Reasoning, logic, interpretation, and analysis are all involved in the activity.

Encourage the Use of Existing Abilities and Interests. Most learners are competent in special areas such as computer graphics, drawing, music, photography, written expression, visual arts, and so forth. Because of their prior success in certain areas, the opportunity to use them in new learning reduces some threat posed by the new subject. Therefore, seek ways to enable learners to address significant learning goals through their pre-existing competence and/or interest.

SUMMARY

This chapter discussed how to prepare individuals for self-directed learning. It was noted that technological advances in information management and communications contain potential for dramatically altering teaching and learning. It was proposed that increasing learner autonomy and self-direction in learning will be more important in education and training in the future.

It was concluded that e-learners and learners using other modes can be prepared for self-directed learning by experience. Two types of experiences were mentioned: serendipitous and planned. This discussion was limited to planned activities that can provide the learner with a successful self-directed learning experience.

The chapter contained two major sections. Based on the assumption that teachers and trainers must have an understanding of the task of preparing for self-directed learning, the first section was designed to discuss some of the conceptual problems and difficulties in self-directed learning. The second part of the first section was concerned with obstacles usually found in the learner's experience. The second, and final, major division focused on preparing learners for self-directed learning. Two strategies, direct and indirect, were discussed. Seven principles that should guide the facilitator regardless of the selected strategy were identified. Specific procedures appropriate to each strategy were briefly presented.

References

Adler, D.A. (1990). *Thomas Alva Edison: A great inventor.* New York: Holiday House.

Dekruif, P. (1926). *The microbe hunters.* New York: Harcourt, Brace.

Dewey, J. (1913). *Interest and effort in education.* New York: Houghton Mifflin.

Edison, T.A. (1971). *The diary of Thomas A. Edison.* Old Greenwich, CT: Chatham Press.

Follett, K. (1989). *Pillars of the earth.* New York: Signet.

Garrison, D.R. (1993). An analysis of the control construct in self-directed learning. In H.B. Long & Associates, *Emerging perspectives of self-directed learning* (pp. 27–44). Norman, OK: Oklahoma Research Center for Continuing Professional and Higher Education, University of Oklahoma.

Graeve, E.A. (1987). *Patterns of self-directed professional learning of registered nurses.* Doctoral dissertation, University of Minnesota, Dissertation Abstracts International, p. 820 48/04A, AAC8709556.

Grow, G. (1991). The staged self-directed learning model. In H.B. Long & Associates, *Self-directed learning: Consensus & conflict* (pp. 199–226). Norman, OK; Oklahoma Research Center for Continuing Professional and Higher Education, University of Oklahoma.

Lewis, H. (1981). *Something hidden: A biography of Wilder Penfield.* Toronto, Ontario: Doubleday.

Long, H.B. (2000). Understanding self-direction in learning. In H.B. Long & Associates, *Practice & theory in self-directed learning* (pp. 11–24). Schaumburg, IL: Motorola University Press.

Long, H.B. (2001). A new era in teaching and learning. In H. B. Long & Associates, *Self-directed learning & the information age* (pp. 1–15). Schaumburg, IL: Motorola University Press.

Massie, R.K. (1980) *Peter the great: His life and world.* New York: Knopf.

Piskurich, G.K. (2001). Developing a system to prepare employees for self-directed interventions. In H.B. Long &Associates, *Twenty-first century advances in self-directed learning* (pp. 30–52). Schaumburg, IL: Motorola University Press.

Quinn, S. (1995). *Marie Curie: A life*. New York: Simon & Schuster.

Ravid, G. (1986). *Self-directed learning as a future training mode in organizations*. Doctoral dissertation, University of Toronto, Dissertation Abstracts International 47/06a, p. 1993, AAC055049.

Smiles, S. (1866). *Self-help*. New York: A.L. Burt.

Straka, G.A., Klienmann, M., & Stokl, M. (1994). Self-organized job related learning: An empirical study. In H.B. Long & Associates, *New ideas about self-directed learning* (pp. 149–160). Norman, OK: Oklahoma Research Center for Continuing Professional and Higher Education, University of Oklahoma.

About the Author

Huey B. Long, Ph.D., was a tenured faculty member at Florida State University, the University of Georgia, and the University of Oklahoma before retiring in 2002. In addition he served as visiting professor at numerous international and American universities between 1975 and 2002. Dr. Long was appointed professor in 1974 and also served as associate dean for research and graduate studies and director of graduate studies, College of Education, The University of Georgia. He was director of the Florida State University Urban Research Center and director of the Oklahoma Research Center for Continuing Professional and Higher Education, University of Oklahoma. Dr. Long has published over seven hundred articles, books, and book chapters.

Chapter 2

Identifying Learners Who Are Ready for e-Learning and Supporting Their Success

Lucy M. Guglielmino and Paul J. Guglielmino

Comments from e-Learners

"I've always learned for myself and it's great that now that's OK."

"I wasn't prepared for how much I had to do on my own."

THE RAPID PROLIFERATION OF E-LEARNING now reaches almost every possible educational setting, from preschool through higher education and into training and development in an incredible variety of settings. It enables the delivery of high-quality, up-to-date, standardized or customized learning throughout the world, with estimates of cost savings of as much as 50 to 70 percent (Burrows, 2002, p. 1). The online training market is expected to nearly double in size annually through 2003, reaching approximately $11.5 billion by that time. Nancy Lewis, director of worldwide management at IBM, comments, "We have been able to provide five times as much content, at one-third the cost, with e-learning" (e-Learning Applications, 2002). Why, then, are some companies and institutions slowing their e-learning expansion? Why have some found high dropout rates in their e-learning offerings?

In a natural reaction to a learning delivery system that promises so much, it appears that the providers of education and training forgot one important component: the learner. Humans tend to need time (and sometimes new skills) to adapt to new learning situations; e-learning is no different. The lack of experience in taking responsibility for one's own learning, the lack of technical skills, and a simple human resistance to change that happens rapidly without transition time or transitional structures have all contributed to the problem. If learners are truly ready for e-learning, it is an efficient, effective, and economical approach. If they are not, the attempt to use e-learning may lead to frustration, battered egos, wasted time, incomplete learning, and program failures.

In addition, learners who are not ready for e-learning but are pushed into it are likely to have a negative experience, which will make them even more resistant to future e-learning opportunities. How can we avoid wasting the resources of the organization, frustrating the learner, and limiting the learners' interest in this promising delivery system? Learning from the mistakes already made, e-learning providers can take the time to determine learner readiness for e-learning before rushing wholesale into e-learning delivery. Once they have addressed the readiness issue, they can further increase the potential for e-learning success by allowing adequate time and attention for e-learning design that respects a variety of learning styles, developing transition structures and support structures for e-learners and ensuring that time for learning and rewards for learning are commensurate with those of other delivery systems.

COMPONENTS OF LEARNER READINESS FOR E-LEARNING

The first component of learner readiness for e-learning that occurs to many people is technical skills. However, the report of a national survey of trainers, professors, and learners involved in online instruction polled through the Distance Education Online Symposium listserv (DEOS-L) concluded that a simple assessment of technical skills as provided by some institutions is not sufficient for an adequate screening and counseling of individuals preparing to participate in electronic distance education classes. While technical skills are certainly important, research and opinion reported in the literature indicate that readiness for self-direction in learning, or the ability to manage one's own learning, is even more vital (Guglielmino & Guglielmino, 2001).

The DEOS survey confirmed that there are two major components of learner readiness for successful e-learning: *technical readiness* and *readiness for self-directed learning*. Each component is composed of specific knowledge, attitudes, skills, and habits (KASH). Knowledge, the first stage of understanding, provides the basic information needed. However, an individual may have the knowledge needed to do something but choose not to. Attitudes are the second major ingredient: an individual's feelings, beliefs, and associated behavioral tendencies arising from both heredity and environment have a strong influence on behavior. Even if an individual's knowledge and attitudes provide a good basis for self-directed learning, they are not sufficient without the necessary skills for implementation. Once the knowledge, attitudes, and skills are in place, formation of positive habits can solidify a successful approach to e-learning (Guglielmino & Guglielmino, 2002).

Technical Readiness for e-Learning

An individual who has the requisite knowledge, attitudes, skills, and habits in technology will have a definite advantage over the novice in terms of readiness for e-learning. The strength and duration of the advantage depends, of course, on the complexity of the technical skills needed.

Technical Knowledge

The technical knowledge needed for e-learning includes a basic knowledge of the components and operations of the technical system being used to deliver the e-learning. In addition, the learner will need to be aware of resources for technical assistance that can be used if problems are encountered.

Technical Attitudes

The major attitude involved in technical readiness for e-learning is a positive feeling about the use of technology as a delivery system for learning—in other words, a lack of technophobia. Other attitudes supporting technical readiness include confidence in one's ability to manage the basic technology involved and a positive expectation in terms of being able to master new technical challenges. For example, an e-learner working in a web-based system might be asked to make the transition from using email to chat rooms or from posting a project to a discussion board to actually presenting it online using Real Player. A positive attitude keeps these technical challenges from becoming roadblocks.

Technical Skills

Obviously, e-learners must be able to competently apply the basic skills needed in order to use the technical system used to deliver the e-learning. For example, a learner using a web-based delivery system would need to have the skills necessary to access the Internet, perform basic email functions, perform basic word processing functions, and use other skills as required.

Technical Habits

Habits contributing to technical readiness would vary with the technology used for the e-learning. Developing habits to ensure appropriate participation, submission of work, and saving of work completed is vital. As an example, if a web-based platform were being used, habits such as maintaining an organized desktop and backing up regularly would be important.

SELF-DIRECTED LEARNING READINESS

The characteristic that is most frequently associated with success in e-learning in the literature is variously referred to as *independence*, *self-direction*, or *autonomy in learning*. e-Learning resources assistant general manager Cleone Bakker recently pinpointed a lack of readiness for self-direction in learning as a problem for e-learners: "In many cases, [people] are used to being 'spoon-fed' their information. Taking responsibility for their own learning may require a change in their mindset" (Burrows, p. 2). Burrows also commented on survey results that showed that only the most motivated and self-disciplined learners thrived on early e-learning courses. These were the self-directed learners.

In 1977, after a nationwide Delphi study on the characteristics of highly self-directed learners, Guglielmino (1977, 1998) proposed a description of a highly self-directed learner:

> A highly self-directed learner, based on the survey results, is one who exhibits initiative, independence, and persistence in learning; one who accepts responsibility for his or her own learning and views problems as challenges, not obstacles; one who is capable of self-discipline and has a high degree of curiosity; one who has a strong desire to learn or change and is self-confident; one who is able to use basic study skills, organize his or her time and set an appropriate pace for learning, and to develop a plan for completing work; one who enjoys learning and has a tendency to be goal-oriented. (p. 73)

The definition suggests a variety of knowledge, attitudes, skills, and habits that comprise readiness for self-directed learning.

SDL Knowledge

A pivotal requirement for readiness for self-directed learning is self-knowledge: an understanding of oneself as a learner based on an honest appraisal. It includes knowledge of one's levels of initiative and persistence and an awareness of one's preferred means of perceiving and processing information. Readiness for self-directed learning also involves an understanding of ways of managing one's own learning. Also critical is the realization that self-direction in learning is a skill that can be learned and further developed.

SDL Attitudes

Attitudes are the central component of readiness for self-direction in learning. The attitudes forming a foundation for success in self-directed or self-managed learning are based in a strong desire to learn or change. The individual who has a strong curiosity, enjoys learning new things, is focused on continuous self-improvement, and views learning as a path to problem solving is likely to be a successful e-learner. A second fundamental attitude is confidence in oneself as a competent, effective learner: seeing oneself as a "can-do" learner and taking the initiative in learning.

Acceptance of Responsibility for One's Own Learning. Accepting responsibility for one's own learning and viewing problems as challenges rather than obstacles are closely related attitudinal components. The successful self-directed learner believes that the primary onus for learning is on the learner. He or she is the one who must recognize needs for learning and take the responsibility for making it happen. This learner will find a way to make the learning occur, regardless of the course design, other inviting activities, unforeseen occurrences—all the distractions that are used by some as an excuse for truncated learning.

Creativity and Independence in Learning . In well-designed e-learning settings, creativity and independence in learning are also crucial. Challenging e-learning settings require the ability to think creatively and develop one's own thoughts and processes for identifying and solving problems rather than simply following directions.

A Willingness to Seek Help. The idea of the self-directed learner as a lone wolf struggling to find answers in isolation is a myth. The effective self-directed learner uses all the tools available, then invents those that are not. Those individuals who are reluctant to ask questions, seek clarification, or solicit expert advice handicap themselves in terms of learning progress. Those who are willing to ask for help reduce the time involved in responding to problems and challenges and avoid frustration that can lead to poor completion rates.

Valuing One's Own Learning. Another important component of self-directed learning is the valuing of one's own learning, a belief in the importance of learning achieved on one's own. The very structure and functioning of our educational system, the nature of credentials required for most employment, and societal practice have unintentionally devalued the learning achieved outside of formal classroom situations, promoting the idea that unless an instructor tells you what to learn, delivers the information to you, and then tests you on it, that learning doesn't count. The expansion of knowledge in the information age makes this concept not only foolish, but potentially damaging: In some arenas, where new challenges and obstacles are being presented daily, if individuals wait for someone else to tell them what to learn, they and their organizations will lag behind instead of leading.

SDL Skills

Logically, basic academic skills are an important part of readiness for e-learning, especially reading skills. Depending on the instructional design, writing skills can also be critical. Self-directed learners are also usually skilled at identifying and analyzing their learning needs. Key skills related to meeting these learning needs include the ability to set learning goals, develop a learning plan, identify resources for learning (both human and material), implement the learning, and evaluate the learning. Time management skills and document or report preparation skills support this process.

SDL Habits

One of the most important habits of the successful self-directed learner is the habit of *persistence*: the refusal to be deterred from reaching a goal because of problems, boredom, or other factors or events that might derail a less determined learner. Habits such as systematic planning, productive organization of learning media and materials, and completing tasks within the time scheduled can streamline and anchor the effective e-learning.

Two other habits are worth emphasizing: the habits of *reflection* and *environmental scanning*. The reflective individual is regularly thinking about events and actions, his or her own performance, possible results of actions or events, how his or her own actions are being interpreted, possible motivations for others' actions, analyzing his or her own learning, learning processes, learning outcomes (meta-learning)—in other words, looking at things from both a macro and a micro view in a search for new insights and meaning. A part of this reflection is environmental scanning, an ongoing, active awareness of changes in the environment and their possible implications, including possible needs for new learning.

IMPROVING THE SUCCESS RATE OF E-LEARNING IN TERMS OF LEARNER PREPARATION AND SUPPORT

Four proven strategies can improve the possibilities for learner success in e-learning environments. First, provide opportunities for learners to assess themselves in terms of technical readiness, readiness for self-directed learning, and preferred learning styles. Then provide follow-up training as needed, provide transition structures to ease the adaptation to the demands and differences of e-learning, and, finally, provide learner support systems that can be easily accessed during the e-learning experience. Some approaches to doing this are described below. Others can be found in the *ASTD Handbook of Training Design and Delivery*, which has a section on self-directed and electronic learning (Piskurich, Beckschi, & Hall, 2000).Then, of course, it is vital that the e-learning design be well-planned and implemented—but that is another chapter.

1. Provide Opportunities for Learner Assessment

Assessment of Learners' Technical Readiness. Many "free," non-copyrighted instruments for assessing technical skills are available on the web; some are very brief, and others are quite complex, including questions related to the use of databases and spreadsheets, the creation of graphics, advanced word processing operations, and the like. Remember: It is pointless to assess readiness on the basis of a wide range of technical skills that may not be needed for a particular course. It is generally agreed that those who are committed to e-learning and are self-directed can learn the specific technical skills needed for a particular learning activity if they already possess basic technical knowledge. As previously mentioned, technical skills are not the central element of readiness for e-learning. Based on a review of the literature, independence, autonomy, or self-direction in learning is even more important. An instrument that includes a basic assessment of technical readiness and also assesses readiness for self-directed learning is discussed in the next section.

If the technical skills required by your e-learning platform are quite complex or advanced, you may want to develop a customized assessment of technical readiness for the specific skills needed.

Assessment of Self-Directed Learning Readiness. Many business organizations and educational institutions have used the Self-Directed Learning Readiness Scale (SDLRS) (Guglielmino, 1977) to assess readiness for e-learning, either in the research form or the self-scoring format: the Learning Preference Assessment (Guglielmino & Guglielmino, 1991). This instrument has proved to be reliable and valid over its twenty-five-year history, and it is the most widely used instrument of its kind (Delahaye & Choy, 2000; McCune, 1988; Merriam & Caffarella, 1999).

The Distance Learning Readiness Assessment (DLRA) is a new assessment instrument designed to more closely target the two major components of readiness for e-learning (technical and self-directed learning readiness). Developed after a national survey of professors and HRD professionals involved in delivering distance learning as well as learners participating in e-learning, it incorporates items from the SDLRS with new items related to technical readiness.

Assessment of Preferred Learning Styles. Learners approach the learning process with different preferred ways of taking in and processing information. While some learning styles assessments offer quite complicated or jargon-filled feedback that many online learners will hesitate to tackle on their own, most learners can easily understand and make appropriate adaptations based on an assessment of perceptual learning styles. Perceptual learning styles are preferred ways of taking in information: auditory, visual, kinesthetic, or interactive. One of the most comprehensive and respected learning styles assessments, by Dunn and Dunn, has a subtest related to perceptual learning styles. It is described in detail at www.unc.edu/depts/ncpts/ publications/learnstyles.htm. A search for the keywords *learning styles* on the Internet will provide a number of other learning style assessments that can be used. While many have not been carefully validated and do not have good levels of reliability, they are still valuable, as they lead the learners to think about their preferred ways of learning. If e-learning participants have an opportunity to assess and reflect on themselves as learners, they will be better able to choose appropriate e-learning options or adapt learning strategies that will help them to master the e-learning content. For example, a learner with a strong preference for interactive learning may choose an e-learning experience that incorporates chat rooms, e-conferencing, or discussion boards rather than one with a strong reliance on gaining information, responding individually to exercises or tests, and getting feedback only from an automatic scoring system. In cases where a variety of options are not available, the learners' knowledge of their learning preferences can assist them in devising techniques to make the learning easier. A learner with a strong aural preference might tape a telecast or video clip to replay as a study aid, while a kinesthetic learner might take notes by hand or on a laptop.

2. Provide Training Where Needed

Technology Training. Obviously, learner success is facilitated if assessed deficiencies are addressed before the experience. A brief session of online training or referral to a class or workshop can assist those whose technology skills do not meet the demands of the specific e-learning activities for which they have enrolled. If it is logistically possible, an excellent beginning for those new to e-learning is a face-to-face introductory session in a computer lab with a real person available to walk them through the technological skills they need; time to try out the skills and become familiar with the e-learning format; and an opportunity to ask questions and receive immediate, hands-on assistance. If a face-to-face session is not possible, an introductory online exercise can be developed to accomplish the same purpose. At a minimum, less experienced e-learners can be paired with co-learners who are more technologically experienced and can serve as mentors.

SDL Awareness Sessions and Training. For those who have lower levels of readiness for self-direction in learning, an awareness session can be a strong impetus to put aside some of the old thought patterns that are often imprinted in formal educational settings. Self-directed learning is a natural process that, in many, has been stifled in teacher-directed classrooms, where the teacher is seen as the guru responsible for learning: telling the learner what to learn, when to learn it, how it will be tested, and then awarding a grade, a certificate, or some other stamp of approval to certify the learning as worthwhile (Guglielmino & Guglielmino, 1991). In actuality, the majority of our most important learning is self-directed: How to deal effectively with relationships, how to solve a problem or develop a new product, how to prepare ourselves for a career or retirement are all self-managed learning projects. A carefully designed intervention can be transformational if it leads the learner to reflect on and challenge some of the roadblocks to self-directed learning.

3. Provide Transition Structures from Traditional Learning to e-Learning

In addition to opportunities for assessment and orientation to new technical skills and self-direction in learning, new e-learners or those with lower levels of readiness for online learning may need additional support in their first learning experiences.

Introduce New Technical Functions Gradually. A learner unfamiliar to an online classroom platform such as Blackboard or Web CT might be overwhelmed if required to use the virtual classroom, group chat, and discussion board functions—all in the first learning activity. The first learning activities should make use of the simpler technical functions, then gradually add the more complex ones, with reference to the available user's manual. As good instructional design moves from simple to complex in terms of content, good instructional design for new e-learners moves from simple to complex technical skills.

Provide Delivery Options That Offer Varying Levels of Support for e-Learners. Learners value the option of having a variety of delivery options to choose from, including traditional, class-based learning; partially class-based, partially e-based; and totally e-based. Many of the problems involved in the introduction of e-learning can be traced to a "sink or swim" or "all or nothing" mentality. Sold on the promises of e-learning effectiveness and economy, some organizations have invested large amounts of money into e-learning design, then simply announced that some learning experiences will only be available in that format. Often completion rates are low or learners' complaints are strident because they were inadequately prepared for the change.

Most learners become accustomed to e-learning with much less stress and far fewer problems if they first have an opportunity to participate in learning experiences which alternate between class-based and e-learning environments. They derive a great deal of psychological comfort from knowing that someone will be available to answer their questions face-to-face at every other session. This psychological support becomes less important as the learner becomes more accustomed to the electronic format and realizes that online interaction can be quite satisfying as well.

Although it has some definite advantages, e-learning is not the best format for everything. Some topics lend themselves better to either class-based or e-based learning formats. For example, learning the principles of conflict resolution or negotiation via e-learning would be very effective, and good e-based simulations might help to build skills, but transfer to practice would be more likely if some face-to-face practice was included.

4. Provide Technical and Content Support

e-Learners dream of an online help desk. The opportunity to obtain both technical and content support on an as-needed basis would be invaluable in ensuring productive learning time. Obviously, this type of support is beyond the reach of some organizations. Less ambitious but still very useful support systems include reference documents of frequently asked questions or ways to resolve typical problems that can be accessed as needed. A search capability for these aids would be a valuable plus.

Even the simplest of support systems can enhance learner success in distance learning. A simple pairing of the less technically skilled with the more technically skilled can greatly reduce frustration.

Learner assessment, pre-training opportunities, and learner support can greatly enhance success rates in electronic distance learning; however, they are not sufficient to ensure success. Good instructional design, reliable technology, appropriate and timely feedback, and many other factors also have a strong impact on success rates in electronic distance learning. Since e-learning holds so much promise in terms of efficiency and cost-effectiveness, it is worth the effort to carefully examine our approaches and outcomes to maximize success.

References

Burrows, T. (2002). *Is e-learning worth the effort?* IT Web: the Technology News Site. www.itweb.co.za. [Posted 14 January 2002, accessed March 4, 2002.]

Delahaye, B., & Choy, S. (2000). The learning preference assessment. In J. Maltby, C.A. Lewis, & A. Hill, *The handbook of psychological tests.* Wales, U.K.: Edwin Mellen Press.

e-Learning applications (2002). www.bitsonline.net/bitsonline.net/bits/e_learn_home.html [Accessed 3/6/2002]

Guglielmino, L.M. (1978). Development of the self-directed learning readiness scale. Doctoral dissertation, University of Georgia. *Dissertation Abstracts International, 38,* 6467A.

Guglielmino, L.M., & Guglielmino, P.J. (1991). *Learning preference assessment.* King of Prussia, PA: Organization Design and Development.

Guglielmino, P.J., & Guglielmino, L.M. (2001) Learner characteristics affecting success in electronic distance learning. In H.B. Long & Associates, *21st century advances in self-directed learning.* Schaumburg, IL: Motorola University Press.

Guglielmino, P.J., & Guglielmino, L.M.(2002). Are your learners ready for e-learning? AMA *handbook of online learning.* New York: American Management Association.

McCune, S.K. (1988) A meta-analytic study of adult self-direction in learning: A review of the research from 1977 to 1987. Doctoral dissertation, Texas A&M University. *Dissertation Abstracts International, 49,* 3237.

Merriam, S., & Caffarella, R. (1999). *Learning in adulthood.* San Francisco: Jossey-Bass.

Piskurich, G., Beckschi, P., & Hall, B. (Eds.).(2000). *The ASTD handbook of training design and delivery.* New York: McGraw-Hill.

About the Authors

Dr. Lucy Madsen Guglielmino is currently professor of adult and community education at Florida Atlantic University in Boca Raton, Florida. She has authored or co-authored more than one hundred publications and is best known for her development of the Self-Directed Learning Readiness Scale (with a self-scoring form known as the Learning Preference Assessment).

Dr. Paul Guglielmino is an associate professor of management at Florida Atlantic University. He teaches undergraduate and graduate level courses in the area of general management, entrepreneurship, and new business formation. In 1998, Dr. Guglielmino was selected University Distinguished Teacher of the Year at Florida Atlantic University. He has served as an advisory board member at Walt Disney World in Orlando and has consulted with companies such as Disney, Motorola, AT&T, Johnson & Johnson, and Medtronic, as well as many other organizations. In 1993 he and a fellow colleague received the Coleman Award for Research Excellence in Entrepreneurial Education at the 38th World Conference on Small Business. Dr. Guglielmino is listed in the *International Directory of Business and Management Scholars*, Harvard University, and is a member of the Academy of Management and a past member of the Academy of International Business. He is a member of Phi Kappa Phi and Beta Gamma Sigma. Dr. Guglielmino has published more than thirty academic articles and book chapters. He is currently writing an authoritative chapter for the American Management Association's handbook on e-learning.

Chapter 3

Utilizing Learning Guides to Maximize e-Learning at Motorola

Richard Durr

Comments from e-Learners

"The study guide gave me something I could read in bed."

"More, and more complete outlines."

"I wanted something to take away from the e-learning, like the stuff you take away from a classroom."

MOTOROLA HAS BEEN RECOGNIZED FOR YEARS in business and industry as a leader in supporting the learning and development requirements of its employees. Motorola established Motorola University in 1981, which was years before most corporations recognized the strategic and performance benefits of a strong organized effort to support employee training and development.

What Motorola University found out in the late 1990s after deployment of an online course delivery system was that only 7 percent of employees who accessed the online training completed the training courses they registered for. Was it because employees did not find the training beneficial? Tests previously conducted verified industry standard results that, when an employee completed an online course, there was relative satisfaction that the content met the training need, the course was easy to use, there was a higher retention rate, and the learner was able to complete the same learning objectives in a shorter period of time than with an instructor-led classroom-delivered course.

So in 1999, Motorola University set out to establish some best practices for using online training in order to address these issues. Credit must be given to Jim Frasier, a former Motorola University manager, for designing and managing the team that undertook the task of researching and documenting some best practices for optimizing e-learning usage at Motorola.

RESEARCH QUESTIONS

As stated earlier, Motorola was only seeing a 7 percent completion rate by employees of the e-learning courses they started. What was just as troubling was that, of those who registered for specific e-learning courses, 69 percent had not even started a course. The three top reasons given for not starting or completing the training were:

1. Did not have time to train at work.
2. Had problems downloading files.
3. Had problems in signing on and using passwords.

It became clear that there were both environmental as well as online system problems leading to low levels of e-learning usage. A series of research questions was formulated to give some direction as to understanding what needed to be done to improve the usage of e-learning and respond to the reasons given for not starting or completing:

- What are the "best practices" for accelerated roll-out and user acceptance of e-learning?

- What is the model, or system, required to create a "best practice" learning environment for e-learning?
- What are the critical elements of the model that will yield the largest return with the smallest investment?
- What is the implementation process for accelerating the worldwide roll-out and increasing user acceptance of e-learning?
- What is the cultural shift and change management process required to accelerate the worldwide roll-out and increase user acceptance of e-learning?

A concept was devised and implemented in a systematic, research-oriented fashion, aimed at resolving the key issues. The concept involved the creation of a "Learning Guide" to provide and offer online assistance to e-learning students. If a Learning Guide were to contact the learner and offer guidance on best practices for e-learning and offer assistance when needed, it was felt the lack of time to train and technical difficulties identified by the learner could be addressed and, hopefully, overcome. Thus, the Learning Guide could be considered by the learner as a contact point, providing assistance in any aspect of support required, whether it be the use of the courseware itself or use of the technology delivering the courseware. From the learners' perspective, the Learning Guide would embody a personality, offering tips, instructions, and ideas on use of the e-learning courses. From the training department perspective, which is responsible for supporting learners, the Learning Guide would consist of any electronic messages, published information, or human contact with an e-learner that would have consistent communication methodologies, giving the learners the sense they have a "personal trainer" to assist them in any aspect of an e-learning engagement.

Other important issues that surfaced from anecdotal evidence regarding use of e-learning were also considered. One was the understanding that, as employees came out of the typical instructor-led classroom environment to achieve their required learning through the formal education system, it is clear that the learning process was a largely other-directed effort. This environment thus became their preference and comfort level for learning. Since e-learning requires the learner to be self-motivated, it was hoped the Learning Guide would be perceived as a similar level of support that a teacher would offer in the traditional classroom setting. Other considerations needing to be remedied were that if an employee was engaged in training at his or her desk, it became difficult for the employee to ignore the work that needed to be done there due to interruptions by the phone or people who dropped in, and/or the learner's manager perceived the employee's workload as insufficient since the employee seemed to have time to do training at the desk. Also, since employees always made time to attend classroom-delivered training and the manager accepted attendance in classroom courses as legitimate time away from the job, it was hypothesized that cultural shifts were required to resolve these issues.

RESEARCH PLAN

An action research methodology was deployed whereby the research team implemented the Learning Guide process and monitored the results simultaneously. No announcement was made or indication offered to the learners while the study was undertaken. Therefore, the subjects never knew they were being studied, making the Hawthorne effect a non-issue. (The Hawthorne effect is where individuals in a study will be aware of the fact they are being studied and will behave or respond differently knowing they are study subjects.)

The Learning Guide process consisted of several steps:

1. When an employee registered for an e-learning course an email message would be sent from the "Learning Guide" that looked like this:

This email is coming to you from Motorola University. Our records indicate that you recently enrolled in NT migration training at your desktop.

MU has four suggestions that will help you to have a more successful training experience. MU recommends:

1. Print out the attached sign. Post the sign on the back of your chair when you are training at your workplace.

2. Turn off or unplug your telephone when training.

3. Schedule training time on your calendar. Then honor your personal commitment to train on the dates and times you schedule.

4. Find a co-worker who is knowledgeable and willing to help you with questions that you may have when you are training.

     OR

If you prefer learning away from your work area, use the attached map to find the location of your facility's Self-Directed Learning Lab.

Right Knowledge Right Now—Happy Training!

2. After four days, another email message would be sent to check the progress of the learner. This message would ask whether he or she was having any difficulty. If so, the Learning Guide was available to assist.

3. To engage the manager in the process, the Learning Guide would send the following email message to the learner's manager:

I am a learning guide for computer-based training at Motorola University. Our records indicate that one of your reports (employee's name) has registered to take NT migration training at his or her work station.

MU research indicates that when managers meet face-to-face with an employee to plan how best to complete training at the desktop, the employee's

• Commitment to complete training is significantly increased.

• Learning cycle time is significantly decreased.

Please take a moment to talk with (employee's first name) and determine how you can help support him or her having a successful experience while training at his or her desktop.

Best regards,

Jim Frasier

MU Learning Guide

Right Knowledge Right Now

4. After four days, the manager would be sent a follow-up email asking whether or not the manager was able to review the employee's e-learning progress and help establish a positive learning environment for the employee.

The research design was established to measure the effect of the Learning Guide on the use of e-learning. Three research groups were defined: a control group consisted of learners who registered for an e-learning course and did not receive email from the Learning Guide. One experimental group consisted of those who registered for an e-learning course and received the email and a follow-up email from the Learning Guide. A second experimental group consisted of managers of learners who registered for an e-learning course and received the email and a follow-up email from the Learning Guide.

The results of the study were as follows:

1. The control group (the group receiving no Learning Guide email) had a 30 percent start rate, or about the same as before the study took place, which was at 31 percent.

2. In the first experimental group (learners receiving email from the Learning Guide):

   • Eleven percent of the learners replied to the Learning Guide after the first email from the Learning Guide.

   • Ninety-five percent of the Learners exchanged email with the Learning Guide after the follow-up email.

3. In the second experimental group (managers of learners receiving email from the Learning Guide):

   • Five percent of the learners' managers replied to the Learning Guide after the first email from the Learning Guide.

   • Sixty-eight percent of the learners' managers exchanged email with the Learning Guide after the follow-up email.

The study also revealed that twenty-four-hour follow-up email from Learning Guide to learner AND learner's manager resulted in

80 percent of learners starting training (compared to the 30 percent start rate of those in the control group who received no email from the Learning Guide); not one manager expressed irritation at the emails or repeated contact by the Learning Guide; and in follow-up interviews, it was found that when the learner's manager becomes involved in discussing training at the employee's desktop, having time to train in the workplace does NOT continue to be a problem expressed by learners.

FINDINGS FROM THE RESEARCH

Establishing the use of a Learning Guide can be a key factor in helping establish an environment that is supportive for desktop e-learning. The fact that an 80 percent start rate for e-learning occurred after receipt of the first Learning Guide email was more success than the research team ever anticipated.

As the findings suggest, when an external influence is placed on an individual to achieve a goal, there is greater likelihood for success. As to the completion rate (which was at 7 percent before this study was undertaken), the research team did not monitor that result. The Motorola University e-learning team managing this research determined that completion rate for e-learning activity was not important. The entire concept around e-learning is to provide the learning when it is needed and what is needed. When learners engage in e-learning activities, they are empowered to get out of it what they need and are not required to complete the course. This fulfills the promise that e-learning has offered all along—to provide the right learning to the individual learner and reduce the amount of time needed to get it (thus a tremendous time savings and increased productivity by using the saved time to do the job they are paid to do).

Another question addressed was how to improve e-learning engagement without spending a lot of money. Use of email as the vehicle to communicate a Learning Guide concept requires almost no cost at all. A program can be written to automatically have the

Learning Guide emails go to registrants as a response to their registration. Since the registration process is electronic, the program would automatically trigger sending the email and follow-up email, requiring no human intervention.

Of significant importance, this research addressed the issue of the cultural shift requirements as e-learning is adopted. Without the support mechanism that the Learning Guide offers (and replaces the teacher in the classroom), a new methodology for learning is foreign to the learner and learner's manager, so one cannot expect them to inherently know how to adapt to the new methodology. This, then, becomes the job of the learning professional—to analyze the situation and determine the best way to introduce new learning methods to the employee population, taking into consideration learning theory and the overall learning environment. Today, learners are required to be more self-directed in their learning activity, but the learning professionals cannot expect the learner to automatically know how to adapt and make best use of the new learning opportunities that are emerging.

Nicholas Negroponte, in his book *Being Digital*, suggests that the paradigm shifts we are facing in going from an analog to a digital world are generational. As we develop more electronic means to educate the population, the concentrated effort to help the population make the transition to using those electronic methods is only required for the current generation of learners. The generation following, already adept at using the latest electronic devices, gadgets, and games, and proficient with the Internet, will not only NOT need the transitional intervention the current generation needs, but will EXPECT to learn using electronic means. This then suggests that the use of the Learning Guide to replace the teacher and educate the manager should only be a short-lived phenomenon. However, as learners become more self-directed in their learning, other even more perplexing issues are emerging for the learning professional to address, many of which we cannot even conceive today.

About the Author

Richard Durr, Ed.D., is a director at Motorola University in Boynton Beach, Florida. He is extensively involved in the deployment of e-learning to the 100,000 employees of Motorola. He has authored and co-authored several articles on self-directed learning modalities for professionals in the workplace and implementation of self-directed learning processes at various workplace locations around the world. He is also an adjunct professor for the Educational Leadership Department at Florida Atlantic University, Boca Raton, Florida.

Chapter 4

Utilizing a Classroom Approach
to Prepare Learners for e-Learning

George M. Piskurich and Janet F. Piskurich

Comments from e-Learners

"It's harder to focus when there is no class."

"We need an in-class lecture at the beginning to show us how it works."

> "One of the most effective ways to introduce and
> train new learners how to learn in an e-learning
> environment is to use the traditional classroom as
> a setting."
>
> *Elliott Masie*

AT FIRST GLANCE the title of this chapter might seem a little strange, as might Elliott's quote. After all, isn't the purpose of e-learning to do away with classrooms? Doesn't it make stand-up training obsolete by providing a more efficient and more effective way for learners to learn? Well. . . . No.

The purpose of e-learning is to provide a learning delivery system that instructional designers and instructors can use when their learners' needs, their organizations' needs, and their own needs can be best addressed by the advantages of an e-learning design.

That said, we will now refuse to debate this point further, as such is not the purpose of this chapter. Its actual purpose is to provide you with a plan for preparing your learners for e-learning that is best delivered in a classroom setting. We are defining a classroom setting for purposes of this chapter as a training delivery in which the facilitator and learners interact simultaneously. This might be in a face-to-face environment, through satellite mediation, or by utilizing synchronous e-learning.

As we proceed through this chapter we'll discuss why the classroom may be your best preparation alternative and what a complete plan for utilizing it looks like. That's not to say that this is the only approach. Your environment may require a scaled-down version of what we are presenting, or possibly a blended solution that includes both face-to-face and distance learning components. Our main points here are that to be a successful e-learner requires learners to take responsibility for their own learning and that the instructor-facilitated classroom is an effective place to develop that responsibility.

Three Steps for Enhancing Self-Direction

The reasons for using a classroom to initiate what is usually a highly individualized approach to learning goes back to concepts that were discussed by Huey Long and Paul and Lucy Guglielmino earlier in this book and that you'll see again in later chapters. They are the concepts of *self-direction* and *self-directedness*.

Experience has taught us that learners who are not strongly self-directed will not succeed at e-learning, while those who are will succeed, in spite of our best efforts to frustrate them with poorly designed programs, unusable technology, and supervisors who aren't interested.

Research cited in the various proceedings of The International Self-Directed Learning Symposium has taught us that to enhance self-direction in our e-learners requires a three-step approach:

1. Preparation;

2. Creating an environment for small self-directed successes; and

3. Developing a support system.

As we'll see, a classroom approach can deliver all three of these aspects.

That's not to say that there aren't other methods for enhancing self-direction in your e-learners. In fact, even within classroom delivery there are variations. For example, your classroom might be held through an audio or video conference call or via satellite, or even as a synchronous e-learning process, although each of these methods has its disadvantages for this task when compared to face-to-face facilitation.

And speaking of synchronous e-learning: If you are an e-facilitator who feels that what we are talking about is strictly for asynchronous activities and that enhanced self-direction is not necessary in your environment, think again. Consider the various distractions that your learners need to direct themselves away from while your class is in progress, or your possible plans to do some blended learning by having them participate through chat rooms or threaded discussions on a bulletin board. Your control is much more limited in a synchronous classroom, and your learners' self-direction to provide their own control is critically important.

Reasons for Using a Classroom Approach

Here are some reasons for using a classroom methodology for preparing your e-learners.

Learner Comfort. For better or worse, your learners understand the classroom and what's expected of them in it. Their learning about self-direction and e-learning will not be interfered with by their trying to understand the learning method itself when they are in a face-to-face class.

Content Control. In a classroom you know exactly what is presented and how. The instructor, not the learner, interprets concepts and other information, so you are sure all your learners are at least hearing what you need them to hear.

Guidance and Support Mechanism. The classroom instructor, and for a critical time the classroom itself, become the learners' support mechanism. As we noted, providing a support process is a key step in enhancing self-directedness.

Organizational Familiarity. Basically, your organization probably understands classroom learning much better than it does e-learning. You won't have as much difficulty explaining to an as-yet-uninitiated management that their employees need to go to a class as you would explaining, for example, that they need to sit down at a computer to learn how to learn.

Chapter Objectives

We hope we've convinced you by now that classrooms are appropriate places for preparing learners for e-learning, so let's look at the objectives for this chapter.

- Identify reasons why learners are not ready for e-learning;
- Describe the concept of self-directedness and its relation to e-learning;
- Discuss classroom strategies for preparing learners to become successful e-learners; and
- Create your own plan for enhancing self-directedness in your learners.

As you can see, we'll continue providing you with background on self-direction, but within the context of a classroom-based process that you can use to enhance it in your learners.

FACTORS RELATED TO
LEARNER PREPAREDNESS FOR e-LEARNING

We've already identified some reasons related to self-direction for why your learners may not be ready for or may not succeed in e-learning. However, it might help if we look at the overall process in terms of all possible factors. Learner preparation for e-learning can be broken down into four categories. We've listed them here along with examples of some of the major factors related to each category.

Institutional

- Quality of course design;
- Ease of use of company systems;
- Effectiveness and thoroughness of company e-learning policy;
- Availability of internal and external motivation (rewards, completion prizes, contests, advancement, and so forth); and
- Availability of multiple learning resources.

Technical

- Ease in starting and using e-learning programs (general introduction, pop ups for sign in);
- Extra start-up support (on-phone facilitator, technology orientation); and
- Continuing help (help function, help desk 24/365).

Management

- Gives the OK and time, and supports the learning.

Individual

- Are they ready to take on responsibility for their own learning?

SELF-DIRECTEDNESS

If you've read the previous chapters of this book, you should have a good idea of what we mean by self-directedness or self-direction. If not, here are a few of our favorite definitions.

- *Self-Directedness:* A psychological state in which you feel you are personally responsible for yourself and your learning.
- *Self-Direction:* The ability and willingness to direct your own learning.
- *Self-Directed Learning Design:* A training design in which employees master packages of pre-determined material at their own pace, without the aid of an instructor.
- *Self-Directed Learning:* A process in which the individual takes the initiative, with or without the help of others, to diagnose his or her own learning needs, formulate learning goals, identify human and material resources for learning, choose and implement appropriate learning strategies, and evaluate learning outcomes.

While all of these definitions are valid, even if a few are contradictory, it is the last one that is most applicable to e-learning, particularly the aspects of the learner taking the initiative and implementing appropriate learning strategies. Without learners who can do these tasks, it's a good bet that your e-learning will fail.

A MODEL CLASSROOM APPROACH

So how do you get your learners to take the initiative for, to start, to be comfortable with, and to complete e-learning? As we noted, one way is through a class that prepares them to be self-directed in their learning.

In this particular method, we use not one class, but four classes spread over a number of weeks and designed to address our three steps of (1) preparation, (2) creating an environment for small self-directed successes, and (3) developing a support system.

It's important to implement the classes over a period that allows time for the small successes to happen and for your support system to take hold.

Following are annotated outlines created from the actual lesson plans for a four-part course that uses this approach.

Session One

The purpose of the first session is to introduce the concept of self-direction and to make sure everyone is discussing the same concept. At the same time it should present your company's particular view of e-learning and a buy-in process that considers the personal and company advantages of self-directed learning.

Even though there is no post-class activity attached to this class, you might want to allow time between it and the second class for individual coaching and unstructured discussion.

I. Introduction
   A. Icebreaker
      Which cartoon character learns most like you?
   B. Ground rules
   C. Objectives
   D. Your objectives

Your purpose in "A" is to engage the learners in thinking about learning styles and the way people learn and also to have a little fun. Figure 4.1 provides some possible objectives for this first session.

Figure 4.1. Possible Objectives for a Session

Objectives

At the end of this session you will be able to:

- Define the concept of SDL

- Discuss why SDL is important to you personally

- Discuss why SDL is important to the organization

- Develop an appreciation of how much SDL you already do

- Determine your SDL readiness level

- Recall various corporate resources that can be utilized in both SDL and non-SDL environments

II. What is SDL?
    A. Think back to something you've learned on your own
    B. Team definition of SDL
    C. Expert definitions
    D. A group definition for today
    E. Self-directed vs. other-directed

Even though they are probably not sure what self-directed learning (SDL) means yet, this section begins by showing your learners that they are already self-directed learners. You can use the questions in the box below to lead them on this discovery. Afterward they will be ready to define SDL in relation to various experts and the needs of the company.

**Think back to something
you recently learned on your own**

(Not because someone told you to but you wanted to)

- Why did you do it?

- How did you do it?

- What was the outcome?

III. Why is SDL important to:
    A. You
    B. The company
    C. Examples of SDL in action

This is where you add the WIIFMs, not only for the learners, but for the company as well. Figure 4.2 shows an example of possible learner WIIFMs.

Figure 4.2. Reasons to Use SDL

Reasons for Using SDL for Personal Development

- In your career you'll need more than your employer provides
- You have individual needs that are impossible to determine by others such as teachers or supervisors
- You need to decrease your potential professional obsolescence Employment for life vs. Employability for life
- You need to grow

IV. Who does SDL?
   Case study

This is a good place to discuss people in your organization and in others as well who are already involved in e-learning and other self-directed activities.

V. Are you ready for SDL?
   A. SDLRS
   B. Some other research information
   C. A summary of self-direction

The Self-Directed Learning Readiness Scale (SDLRS), discussed in detail in Chapter 2 of this book, is a good tool to use here. However, there are other tools you might employ as well, depending on your particular needs. Here is a list of some major ones, with contact information if you want to follow up on them:

- Self-Directed Learning Readiness Scale (SDLRS). *www.guglielmino.com*. Analyzes individuals' readiness for self-direction through a comparison of the behaviors of highly self-directed individuals.

- Learner Autonomy Profile (LAP). *www.hrdenterprises.com*. Considers four important learner self-directed characteristics: learner desire, resourcefulness, initiative, and persistence.
- Self-Directed Learning Check. *typepress@naxs.net* *(423–733–2025)*. Subdivides learner self-directed characteristics into organizing, reflecting, collaborating, personalizing, doing, observing, envisioning, and imagining.
- Self-Directed Learning Perception Scale. *www.prolt.com*. Emphasizes the learning environment, not the individual learner.

Session Two

The second class introduces the learners to the skills that need to be mastered or augmented to be successful as self-directed learners. It includes a pre-test, much more detailed objectives, and a comprehensive skills-building process. One of the key aspects here is the SDL resource list developed by the company and enhanced by the participants.

The learning plan created at the end of the session, and implemented between this and the next class, is done in conjunction with the participants' supervisors. It functions as a mini-SDL project in keeping with our step of "Creating an environment for small self-directed successes."

I. Introduction
   A: Icebreaker
       Why you feel you are/not a self-directed learner
   B. Ground rules
   C. Objectives
   D. Your objectives
II. Pre-test

This is actually a pre/post test, designed to help the learners think about and then master some SDL concepts. An example of one is located as an addendum to this chapter.

III. Revisiting the SDLRS
  A. Key behaviors

A review here of the key self-directed behaviors that the learn-ers analyzed in the SDLRS that prepares them for the discussion to come.

IV. Abilities needed for self-direction in business

These four abilities are the framework for what the learners will master in the rest of the program, shown in Figure 4.3. They should be discussed in detail.

Figure 4.3. Four Abilities

Abilities Needed for Self-Direction in Business

The ability to:

- Identify and define a problem/learning need
- Find and critique resources for solving the problem/meeting the need
- Capture and apply information from these resources
- Evaluate the success of the process

V. What kind of self-directed learner are you?

Following up on the discussion begun in the introductory ac-tivity in Session One, this area goes into more detail about learning styles, particularly as they relate to learning on your own and e-learning in general. You can use any good learning style inventory here to help your learners understand how they learn best.

VI. Strategies for self-direction
    A. What is an SDL strategy?
    B. A self-directed learning model
    C. The importance of planning
    D. SDL resources
    E. Looking at the situation from multiple points of view
    F. A four-step model for self-direction
    G. Strategies others have found useful

In this area the learners explore how they can become self-directed and the resources available to them. Various models are presented, and a lot of the time is spent allowing them to explore, both in breakout groups and individually, the strategies that best fit their learning style and needs.

Figures 4.4 and 4.5 provide examples of possible strategies and resources that you can suggest to your learners.

Figure 4.4. Sample Strategies

> **Top 10 Strategies for SDL**
>
> - Just think on it (reflection)
> - Ask someone who knows
> - Read books
> - Ask someone who has good ideas
> - Go to a class
> - Use CBT
> - Find a tutor
> - Try doing something
> - Use the WEB
> - Discuss with a group

Figure 4.5. Sample Resources

Self-Directed Learning Resources

- Mentors
- Friends
- Co-workers
- Supervisors
- Customers
- Audio tapes
- Books
- Learning library
- Videotapes
- Books
- CBT programs
- Magazines
- Manuals

- Experimentation
- Observation
- Company courses
- Lectures
- Workshops
- College courses
- Internet
- Company net
- Public library
- Television
- Radio
- Procedures
- Telephone

VII. Obstacles and barriers to self-direction
   A. What might they be?
   B. Compiled list
   C. How do you deal with them?

This is one of the most important aspects of the program. A significant cause of failure for e-learning initiatives is the barriers that companies inadvertently allow to form between the e-learner and program completion. A truly self-directed learner can overcome many of these barriers, particularly if he or she is prepared for them. In this section you want to find out what those barriers (both perceived and real) are for your learners and help them to find ways to overcome them. Figure 4.6 gives you an example of some of these barriers as determined by other groups of learners.

Figure 4.6. Obstacles and Barriers

Obstacles and Barriers to SDL

- Fear of failure (lack of self-confidence)

- Feelings of frustration or inadequacy about learning

- Complex work/life issues

- Learning needs not known or knowable

- Strong management control toward training

- Time

- Lack of management support

- Money

- Interruptions

VII. The SDL learning plan
    A. Ten questions to answer
    B. Example of a learning plan

The final aspect of the second session is the creation of a self-directed learning plan. This plan is completed during the period between the second and third sessions and begins the learning support relationship between the learner and the supervisor. It also provides one of those small self-directed successes you are looking for and prepares your learners for taking control of their own learning. An example of a learning plan can be found in Figure 4.7.

Figure 4.7. Sample Learning Plan

Learning Objectives What do I need to know or be able to do?	Learning Process What steps will I need to take?	Resources What resources will I need?	Possible Obstacles and how to overcome them	Target Dates When will I complete each step?	Evaluation I will have succeeded in my learning when . . .

Session Three

The third session is designed to take advantage of the post-classroom work of the second session in a "learn from the experiences of your colleagues" environment. It still provides instructor support, but it is now moving the participants away from a reliance on an instructor orientation and more toward a self-directed approach, gaining learning resources from wherever they can be found.

I. Introduction
   B. Some thought questions
      1. Have you become more aware of the things you are learning both at work and at home?
      2. Have you been thinking more about how you learn and about what you need to learn?
      3. Have you noticed others around you engaged in self-learning projects?
   B. Today's objectives

The objectives for this session are much broader as the learners move toward creating their own learning objectives as they need them. Figure 4.8 provides some possible objectives.

Figure 4.8. Sample Objectives

Today's Objectives

At the end of this session you will be able to:

- Analyze the success of your SDL learning plan

- Discuss your manager's role in supporting SDL in your workplace

- Create effective SDL contracts with your manager

II. Review and reports on learning plans

In this area the learners discuss as a group how their attempt to complete their learning plans went. Resources used and barriers encountered and overcome are the key aspects here. The participants should be learning from their colleagues' experiences, thus burnishing their own self-directedness as they pick and choose the lessons that will serve them best. This area in turn sets up the discussion for Part III.

III. Working with your manager in a self-directed environment
    A. What do you need from your manager and how do you get it?

The most important resource (and possible roadblock) to e-learning is the learner's manager. Some of the learners will have found this out through the post-activity for Session Two and will relate their stories of triumph and frustration. The question asked above is the key to the discussion. Figure 4.9 provides some follow-up questions you can use to enrich the discussion.

Figure 4.9. Discussion Questions

Working with Your Manager

- How can your manager help you in your self-directed learning process?

- How might your manager inhibit your ability to function as a self-directed learner?

- What techniques can you use to help your manager help you?

IV. The SDL contract
  A. General questions
    1. What group/individual goals am I trying to achieve?
    2. How is this tied into company goals?
    3. What do I need to change to meet the goals?
    4. What do I need to learn to make the changes?
    5. What are my learning objectives?
    6. What methods will I use?
    7. What resources do I need?
    8. How will my success be measured?
       Application to my job
       Effect on goals
  B. Review contract
  C. Role plays

In this particular methodology, everything leads up to this aspect, the creation of an SDL contract. This is the mechanism that will allow your learners to carry on in a self-directed manner, yet still fulfill the learning needs of the organization. The major difference between the learning plan and the contract is the requirement of tying the proposed learning to corporate goals. Once again the supervisor plays a major role in the development of the contract, as well as a resource role as needed by the learner.

Using the contract, your learners can plan both time and opportunity for their e-learning, thus overcoming two serious roadblocks that have been reported by other e-learners. An example of an SDL contract can be found in Figure 4.10.

V. Post-test

The post-test helps to reinforce both the terminology and importance of self-direction. By the completion of this session your learners should be ready to begin working closely with their managers in a self-directed environment to take full advantage of your e-learning offerings and help you accomplish your e-learning goals.

Figure 4.10. Self-Directed Learning Contract

Learner _____

Manager _____

Topic _____

Date Begun _____

Date Completed _____

Organizational Goal This Learning Will Help Achieve	Personal Goal This Learning Will Help Achieve	Learning Objectives (What will I know or be able to do?)	Learning Process (What steps will the learner take?)	Learning Resources (What will we each provide?)	Target Dates	Evaluation (The learner will have succeeded when . . .) (Job application)

_____

Manager's Signature

_____

Learner's Signature

Session Four

Session Four is designed for the learners' managers. Their understanding of the SDL process is critical for both immediate learner support and the long-term continuation of the process. Attending the learners' sessions, or at least an executive overview of them in conjunction with this program, will help your managers prepare for their role in the e-learning process. They will be able to better understand where their learners will be coming from when they ask for help and will be more effective in assisting in the development of the learning contracts.

While we've numbered this class Session Four, the sessions are not necessarily sequential. Managers should usually participate in this session after they have attended the first of the learner sessions or the overview.

    I. Introduction
       Objectives
   II. Why are we thinking about SDL? (management point of view)
     A. Case studies

The WIIFMs for both managers and the organization are discussed here. There are a number of available case studies that show the effectiveness of employees who are self-directed and you can pick or choose the ones that fit your situation. Figures 4.11 and 4.12 provide some possible management WIIFMs.

Figure 4.11. Importance of SDL for Organization

Why SDL Is Important to the Organization	
• Change	• Technology
• Information	• Training people
• Productivity	• Learning organization

Figure 4.12. Importance of SDL for Managers

Advantages of SDL for Managers

- Fewer performance problems

- Fewer tactical questions

- More satisfied employees

- Better trained employees

- More productive employees

- You become proactive, not reactive

- A long-term investment

III. The manager as gatekeeper for SDL
    A. Degree of tension over management control
    B. Entry training vs. development
    C. How do you know who needs support?
    D. Watch out for the employees who always seem to create self-defeating, non-learning experiences.
    E. Tying SDL to business goals
    F. Ideas on where to get information on corporate learning needs (and resources)

This section deals with one of the two overarching responsibilities of the manager in a self-directed, e-learning environment. As *gatekeeper* the manager provides guidance for choosing and initiating e-learning activities. An important aspect here is helping managers to see how to tie the e-learning to business goals. Figure 4.13 provides a summary of learner characteristics that the manager can look for as he or she begins to support the self-directed process.

Figure 4.13. Learner Characteristics

Learner Characteristics

- Desire to learn
  - Not wishing but actively pursuing
- Resourcefulness
- Initiative
  - Requires an authority figure
- Persistence
  - Overcome obstacles

IV. Establishing an SDL environment
- A. Permission
- B. Provide resources
- C. Become a learning coach
- D. Reward success
- E. Reduce fear of failure
- F. Support for learning outcomes
- G. Establish learning groups
- H. Model it yourself
- I. Leave time for thinking (reflection)
- J. Look for informal learning possibilities
- K. Be a manager of learning, not just an information provider

The manager's other major responsibility in working with self-directed learners is to create an environment in which they can succeed. This requires performance of a number of different tasks and often a change in how managers see their own learning support role. They should find themselves moving more towards the role of a learning coach. Another important task is to reward learning successes. Figure 4.14 provides some possibilities for this particular task.

Figure 4.14. Ways to Reward Success

Rewarding Learning Success

- Create a culture that prizes learning
  - Talk about it
- Find incentives for sharing learning
  - Coach or mentor others
  - Have them give a class
  - Write an article
- Special lunch
- APEX nominations
- Peer recognition
  - Sharer/learner of the month
  - Special events
  - Group e-mail
  - Newsletters (e-newsletters)
  - "For learners only" functions with more learning

V. The SDL contract
   A. Why?
   B. Disadvantages
   C. Review of contract
   D. Role plays

The final aspect of the managers' session is to introduce them to the SDL contract from their point of view. Of course the "why's" and the disadvantages will be different from the learners' to some extent, but the similarities are just as important and need to be stressed. Possible reasons why and disadvantages can be found in Figures 4.15 and 4.16.

Figure 4.15. Advantages of Learning Contracts

Why Learning Contracts?

- Get understanding and agreement on objectives
- Get employee involved in planning the learning
- Utilize more and better learning resources
- Create employee accountability for learning
- Encourage personal growth, self-esteem, and confidence in own abilities

---

Figure 4.16. Disadvantages of Learning Contracts

Disadvantages of Learning Contracts

- Not always suitable for performance enhancement training
- Difficult for people who are dependent or unmotivated
- Requires for many a change in their attitude about learning
- One more thing to do for managers
- Managers may need to enhance own skills to manage effectively

---

SUMMARY

The purpose of this systematic, classroom-based approach to preparing learners for e-learning is to enhance the e-learners' self-directedness. This is done by creating a program that addresses the three enhancement aspects of preparation, creating an environment for small self-directed successes, and developing a support system—all are key to enhancing self-direction in learners.

The approach uses a series of activities that introduce the concept of being self-directed to the learners, allow them to practice self-direction in a controlled environment, and provide them with the tools to succeed in self-direction back on the job.

It is certainly not the only approach, nor the best in every situation, as it requires a commitment of time and resources that the organization may not be willing or able to provide. However, you can use the overall concept and pieces and parts of the design to create an e-learner preparation program that fits the specific needs of your organization.

References

Cox, J.H. (1982, March). A new look at learner-controlled instruction. *Training & Development*, pp. 90–94.

Hammond, M., & Collins, R. (1991). *Self-directed learning: Critical practice*. New York: Nichols/GP Publishing.

Hiemstra, R., & Sisco, B. (1990). *Individualizing instruction*. San Francisco: Jossey-Bass.

Kearsley, G. (1985). *Training for tomorrow: Distributed learning through computer and communications technology*. Reading, MA: Addison-Wesley.

Knowles, M.K. (1980, May). How do you get people to be self-directed learners? *Training & Development*, pp. 96–99.

Long, H. (1989). Truth unguessed and yet to be discovered. In H. Long & Associates (Eds.), *Self-directed learning: Emerging theory and practice*. Tulsa, OK: University of Oklahoma Press.

Long, H. (1990). Changing concepts of self-direction in learning. In H. Long & Associates (Eds.), *Advances in research and practice in self-directed learning*. Tulsa, OK: University of Oklahoma Press.

Piskurich, G. (1985). *A partially centralized and partially decentralized training system in a health care setting*. Ann Arbor, MI: University Microfilms International.

Piskurich, G. (1991, September). Ensure quality and quality training through Self-directed learning. *Training & Development*.

Piskurich, G. (1993). *Self-directed learning: A practical guide to design, development, and implementation*. San Francisco: Jossey-Bass.

Rowntree, D. (1986). *Teaching through self-instruction*. London: Kogan Page.

Young, D. (1986). *An exploratory study of the relationship between organizational climate and self-directed learning among organizational managers*. Kansas City, MO: University of Missouri Press.

ADDENDUM

Pre/Post Test

1. In self-directed learning the individual
    A. Formulates learning goals
    B. Has control over how the learning occurs
    C. Has the chance to choose
    D. All of the above
2. True or false
    A. SDL can be important to you as a means of personal development
    B. Many of the reasons that SDL is important to organizations are the same as why it is important to individuals
3. Many people
    A. Practice more SDL at home than at work
    B. Never use SDL at all
    C. Learned how to use SDL in school
    D. Are very familiar with SDL but don't like it
4. True or false
    A. If you score low in SDL readiness you should not attempt to practice SDL
    B. As you get older you tend to lose the ability to practice SDL
    C. A key ability for self-directed learners is the ability to find resources
5. If you are a highly reflective self-directed learner
    A. You'll work well in a team
    B. You'll see various learning alternatives easily
    C. You'll have problems planning your learning
    D. All of the above
6. True or false
    A. The best learning style for SDL is an observing style

Answers

1. D
2. T, T
3. A
4. F, F, T
5. B
6. F

About the Authors

George Piskurich is an organizational learning and instructional design consultant specializing in e-learning design, performance improvement analysis and interventions, and telecommuting initiatives. With over twenty years of experience, he has been a classroom instructor, instructional designer, and corporate training director. He has developed classroom seminars, multi-media productions, and distance learning programs.

Piskurich has been a presenter at over thirty conferences and symposia, including the International Self-Directed Learning Symposium and the ISPI and ASTD international conferences. He has authored books on learning technology, self-directed learning, instructional design, and telecommuting, edited books on instructional technology, HPI, and e-learning, and written many journal articles and book chapters on various topics. He can be reached at (478) 405–8977, by email at Gpiskurich@CS.com, or through his website: GPiskurich.com.

Janet F. Piskurich, Ph.D., is a research scientist and educator on the faculty at Mercer University School of Medicine in Macon, Georgia. Although heavily involved in research related to the control of immune responses, she also tutors first- and second-year medical students in several phases of the biological science curriculum and is involved in teaching various workshops for both children and adults. Her interest in self-direction in learners is reflected by the problem-based learning methodology she employs in her teaching.

Along with numerous scientific publications, she has authored articles and book chapters on self-directed learning and individualized career development. She holds a bachelor of science degree from the University of Pittsburgh and a doctorate in experimental pathology and immunology from Case Western Reserve University, Cleveland, Ohio. She can be reached at (478) 301–4035 or via email at Piskurich_J@Mercer.edu.

Chapter 5

Preparation for e-Learning

A View from a Corporate Learning Leader

Rick Rabideau

Comments from e-Learners

"e-Learning just isn't our priority."

"My boss doesn't believe I'm working."

"They never give me time to sit down and do it."

"I've always learned for myself, and it's great that now that's OK."

"I wasn't prepared for how much I had to do on my own."

THE GREAT CONTRIBUTION OF E-LEARNING to organizations is sustainable competitive advantage through a continuous, just-in-time, and just-for-me learning process. It is an important organizational enabler to be embraced and leveraged by business learning professionals. With the emergence of e-learning, we now have the means to provide high-quality learning solutions within the context of the work itself. These contextual-based learning experiences will impact competitive advantage by increasing learning retention rates and potentially providing a dramatic increase in the transfer from learning to performance.

Successfully implementing e-learning requires a systemic rethinking of a company's learning program. As business learning professionals, we must look at the opportunities e-learning presents in the multi-faceted context of the organization to find a systemic formula that meets the needs for the short term and allows the learning strategy to evolve with coming advances in learning design, development, delivery, and evaluation. This chapter will share lessons we've learned at Prudential Financial in our quest to mine the promise of e-learning.

BACKGROUND

Learning solutions are provided in a variety of ways to the sixty thousand employees of Prudential Financial. The primary means is via collaboration between the business learning teams and a centralized learning organization called Associate Development. The business learning teams provide learning solutions that meet the unique business needs. They leverage the enterprise-wide technical infrastructure and courses provided by the Associate Development team to augment the local curricula.

In 2001 we migrated to a new learning management system (LMS) and with that event dramatically increased the number of e-learning courses available to our associates to nearly two hundred. Our technical addition in 2002 is a learning content management system (LCMS) that will ultimately provide an enterprise-wide design and development platform for e-content. The philosophy and tools for learning are changing at Prudential Financial as we strive to create a learning environment to match the evolving needs of a knowledge-based business in a dynamic environment.

Introduction of these systems has taught us much about the systemic nature of changing the expectation of learners from a classroom-only training model to a learning model that is more blended and self-directed. We are also experiencing a renewed spirit among the business learning teams and Associate Development as the opportunities and challenges inspire us to collaborate and depend on one another to achieve a common good. It is from this systemic perspective that this chapter addresses the challenge of preparing e-learners in a corporate environment.

THE ORGANIZATION: PREPARING THE E-LEARNING ENVIRONMENT

Technology's impact on learning is just beginning; wherever there is a gap with a potential profit, an innovative technologist will find a way to provide a better, faster, less expensive technology solution. During the coming years, business learning professionals will continue to benefit from technical solutions that will enable business learning to be more effective and faster, and with dramatically better results.

It is important that business learning professionals consider these technical solutions carefully as accelerated change reduces the half-life of knowledge, and each year more technically savvy professionals enter our workforces expecting interactive and on-demand learning activities. Concurrently, customers are demanding smarter products that provide greater convenience from companies that provide 100 percent perfect service. The benefits of e-learning match well with these expectations, making its advancement certain.

Figure 5.1 illustrates one perspective of the lifecycle transition between classroom-based training and e-learning. It was developed from insights gained from the article, "Growing Up Digital" by John Seeley Brown of Xerox PARC (Brown, 2002).

Figure 5.1. Learning Lifecycle Perspective

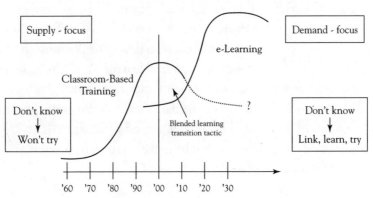

The graphic illustrates the successive life cycles of classroom-based training with the emergence of e-learning. Currently we are in a transition period between the two dominant learning methodologies. What is emerging from this transition is a phase popularly called "blended" learning. This is a transition strategy that leverages the best of both worlds as we augment classroom training with more e-learning solutions. The recipe for the learning blend will consistently change as e-learning design, development, and delivery methods improve. The industry is already producing technical solutions for the aspects of classroom-based training that we cherish, such as collaboration, problem solving, interaction, and questioning. In the next few years distance-learning technologies, learning content management systems, simulation templates, virtual collaboration networks, and the technology-savvy employees who are comfortable using these technologies will become more commonplace in most organizations. The trend is compelling; e-learning will continue to grow in importance as an integral part of a new business learning system.

The figure also shows the transition from a supply-focused training model to one that is demand-focused. The majority of learning continues to be provided via a "supply" of classroom courses that people register for and take in a sequential manner away from their workplace. The predominant trend in business learning is to develop the ability to use technology-based, adaptive learning models that are mapped to reusable learning objects, providing a learning solution adapted to the unique needs of the learner. This system enables a "demand" focused learning process that is capable of providing a structured solution for the employee who is new-to-position, yet flexible enough to provide quick, customized learning nuggets to support an experienced performer with a quick task refresher.

This is a highly probable future scenario for business learning, and company leaders will look to learning professionals to create the vision and strategy to evolve to such a system to support the organization's strategic goals.

The figure also shows the transition in worker empowerment. In many organizations if workers "don't know" how to do a particular task they too often "won't try." Organizations are continually setting higher expectations for performance, providing tools to empower workers for situations when they "don't know" something, and—through technology—enabling them to "link, learn, and try." What they link to are performance support tools . . . learning that is delivered just-in-time and just-for-me.

One other insight illustrated by the figure is that e-learning is in its infancy. The revolution in technology-based learning is just beginning and will continue to provide more and better learning solutions.

It is clear the science is in place to do great new things to improve the corporate learning paradigm, but business leaders and learning professionals need more practice in the art of using these e-learning tools.

E-LEARNING IMPACTS EVERYTHING

In preparing the e-learner it is critical to review and update the systems and processes that provide your organization's learning activities. Ultimately, accommodation of e-learning solutions will require a thorough review of your learning program. From the instructional systems design model to the delivery mechanisms, from learning professional skills to the expectations of learners, there are few systems and processes that will emerge from the transition to e-learning in their present form.

Acquiring e-Learning Knowledge and Skills

e-Learning comes with much new jargon and many technical considerations. Without a technical background, this can be daunting and confusing. If the technical aspects confound you, there are several options to gain support and develop your proficiency.

Develop a strong partnership with your corporate IT department, in particular the networking team. It will be an easy transition for them to apply their knowledge and skill to the field of learning. They will be able to explain the technical infrastructure issues around bandwidth, system configurations, software versions, plug-ins and more. You will need to depend on your corporate IT department throughout the process.

Another approach is to hire the technical skills into your learning department. This will make your transition easier and will likely reduce some of the uncertainty and risk.

You will find several very good training organizations that have developed courses for learning professionals addressing the implementation and delivery of e-learning. Keep an eye on your mail and the trade journals; they advertise regularly.

A wonderful free source is the Internet. Try setting aside a regular time to surf topics or companies that interest you. There are several websites dedicated to e-learning, such as the following:

- www.internettime.com/e.htm—Founded in 1998 to help organizations learn and provide hands-on advice on implementing e-learning.
- www.e-learningguru.com—A comprehensive site with articles, tools, white papers, and more.
- www.learningcircuits.org—ASTD's site features a rich archive of articles and tools.
- www.elearningpost.com—Daily news about the activities in the e-learning world.
- www.lguide.com—Subscription service for many reviews of e-learning courses and resources.
- www.linezine.com—An interesting collection of interviews and articles on a number of relevant themes.
- www.learnativity.com—A wealth of e-learning and related resources.

- www.masie.com—A variety of resources and services.
- www.brandon-hall.com—This site provides a number of research reports (for a fee) and resources.

In addition, there are several monthly publications, including:

- www.onlinelearningmag.com—Search their archives for free.
- www.elearning.com—Archives, resources, and information.
- www.trainingmag.com—Many e-learning resources, archives, and reports.

Most vendors also have websites, many with useful white papers about e-learning strategy and emerging technologies.

e-Learning conferences are another means for developing your knowledge and skills. There are many throughout the year and in all parts of the country. If you can't make it to a conference, plan your own. Identify a few of the vendors who have products you're interested in and invite them to a staff meeting or any gathering of learning professionals. If you are unfamiliar about where to start, ask colleagues in another part of your organization or at a professional association meeting. Vendors are a great free source of current information, and you can be comfortable in asking them almost any question.

These are not mutually exclusive suggestions; you will likely need to do all of them. e-Learning is a new and continually evolving competency area for business learning professionals, and staying up-to-date with the changes will be a constant process.

Changing Processes to Accommodate e-Learning

Many sound and time-tested processes will need to be revised during the transition to e-learning. Here are a few to watch for:

Learning Program Adaptation

e-Learning has the ability to bring learning closer to the work. Below is a sample matrix (Figure 5.2) that may help you envision and communicate where e-learning will serve the organization best.

Figure 5.2. e-Learning Serving the Business

	Sales & Customer Relations	Customer Services	Management
New to Position ~30%	• Structured on-boarding • Blended learning model • SOJT • Emphasis on perf. feedback • Use of e-tools for JIT support	• OTJ—observation • Blended model for job skills • SOJT to proficiency • e-Roleplaying • Use of e-tools for JIT support	• Structured on-boarding • Blended learning model • SOJT • Emphasis on perf. feedback • Use of e-tools for JIT support
Proficient Performers ~70%	• Performance observation and coaching • Assess to ensure consistency • Frequent perf. feedback • Use of e-tools for JIT support • Structured training for new products, processes, or systems	• Observational assessment for consistency and excellence • Team development plans • Use of e-tools for JIT support • Mentoring • Structured training for new products, processes, or systems	• Assess to ensure basic skills excellence • Annual 360 deg. feedback, mid-year upward feedback • Use of e-tools for JIT support • Structured training for new products, processes, or systems

The figure illustrates a conceptualization of a blended learning model and how it can be applied differently to the two major audiences: new-to-position and experienced performers. On an annual basis, organizations have about 30 percent of their workforce who are new-to-position due to new hires, promotions, and job changes. The remaining 70 percent of workers form the key audience of experienced performers, an extremely critical group that accounts for most of the organization's productivity.

For the structured learning needs of the new-to-position group, e-learning is integrated into a blended learning model. The blend of classroom, e-learning, performance support tools, and on-the-job learning allows for the planned integration of e-learning components into a course to leverage its strengths with the benefits of other learning methodologies. This approach provides the new-to-position employees with the structure they need to achieve proficiency quickly. It also prepares them, by reinforcing the use of the just-in-time tools, to learn to become self-initiated and self-directed learners.

The learning needs of the experienced performer group are very different from those of the new-to-position group. These employees are experienced; they are doing the job every day and the company needs them on the job as much as possible. Occasionally, however, even the most experienced performers face situations that are new or unfamiliar; when this happens it is likely they don't need a course, but rather need an answer to a question. In the past, using a 100 percent classroom model, the learning activity was not available immediately, so employees worked around the problem, did it wrong, or interrupted an expert, supervisor, or co-worker. Or if a class was available, the worker had to attend the entire session. With a classroom model, there is limited opportunity to select the portion that addresses the worker's unique performance challenge. This is undesirable in today's highly productive business environments.

Contracting

Using outside vendors to develop instructor-led content is a familiar practice for most business learning professionals. With e-learning, it is almost certain an outside developer will be needed, especially in the beginning. Engaging a vendor for e-learning is more like contracting for software development than for courseware. One suggestion is to visit your corporate IT department and ask them to review their process and requirements for software development with you. You can then make some refinements to their process to meet the unique aspects of e-learning. Particularly noteworthy is the extended timeline for design, development, and testing. e-Learning activities take much longer to design and develop than do instructor-led courses, and there are fewer shortcuts.

Here are a few lessons we've learned about contracting with outside developers for e-learning:

- Seek a company that serves your area and has a good reputation for service.
- Make sure the developer has previously loaded its content successfully into the LMS system you use.
- Ask for a demonstration of previously developed e-learning content.
- Include at least a thirty-day period to make final changes to the content as part of the original agreement.
- Be cautious of "time and material" pricing arrangements.

Consult with your legal department as well. The standard contract for e-learning development is different than the standard contract used for classroom training. The language in your software development contracts will serve as a good starting point for an e-learning contract.

Standards

Establishing standards is an important aspect of transitioning to e-learning. The learning leadership must determine the following:

- The instructional design process to follow;
- The course navigation approach, look, and feel;
- The tools that will be used to ensure authoring compatibility across the company; and
- The formats to ensure the smooth transition of your e-content to the LMS.

For instance, at Prudential Financial our current effort to implement a learning content management system, LCMS, is best served by creating an enterprise-wide design standard. We are working with our business learning colleagues to establish standards that will allow for the exchange and reuse of the learning objects produced by the various business units.

If standards are not established early, the opportunity to take advantage of the economies of scale for e-learning will be difficult. Once the business units establish their own standards and large investments in the development of learning assets are made, it is an arduous and time-consuming process to sort out the issues and reverse-engineer a single standard.

Testing and Quality Assurance

The testing and quality assurance process for e-learning is a critical step in preparing the environment for e-learners. In addition to testing the effectiveness of the instructional aspects, there are several technical tests that must be performed to ensure a quality end result. For instance:

- Usability testing, which ensures every button works, every interaction is complete, and every reinforcement and response is accurate.
- Functional tests on the various hardware configurations and software versions used in your organization. For example, at Prudential Financial we've identified nine different system

configurations that often must all be accommodated by our testing process.

- Stress testing the network to ensure it can withstand a large number of learners making requests simultaneously.

- It is also critical to test the data transfers for book marking, course completion, and assessments from the course to the LMS.

In total these tests may take from a week or two to many weeks. Testing is important and requires collaboration between the developer, the learning team, and the corporate IT department. Problems usually occur if technical standards are not adhered to or if content providers/developers are unfamiliar with your LMS; either situation can create a cycle of test, modify, test, modify . . . a time-consuming, costly, and frustrating process.

The testing and quality assurance (QA) process will also require support from your IT department. It is best to contact them early on for their suggestions and requirements on how to establish an efficient process. They may likely have a QA lab established, staffed with software testing experts, and you may be able to work out an arrangement to leverage those resources.

At Prudential Financial we've addressed each of these issues, some proactively and some without the luxury of unlimited time. We've reaffirmed the wisdom of tackling these system and process issues early to avoid service problems with our e-learners.

Pricing for e-Learning

One of the responsibilities for the corporate learning team at Prudential Financial is to provide e-learning content for topics that broadly apply to all of the business units, such as business skills, professional skills, finance, and corporate citizenship. For most of this content, we license courses from content vendors. In the past year we've been asked to attribute costs directly to the business unit that utilizes the service. As such, in 2002 we established a nominal charge-back fee for the first launch of an e-learning course (subsequent launches of the same course by a learner are free). This allows us to distribute the licensing costs fairly while keeping the cost to the departments very low. Proprietary e-learning courses developed by the business units are usually provided with no fee to the learner.

This approach appears to be fundamentally sound, although we've noticed a decrease in the number of launches from 2001, when there was no charge, to 2002. There are two possible explanations:

1. The 2001 usage rate is likely inflated because there was no downside for employees launching many offerings looking for something interesting.

2. Having a fee, however nominal, is a barrier to allowing team members to access the commercially licensed e-learning courses.

One other insight that has emerged is the ongoing need to have someone to manage the e-learning content portfolio. For instance, a team member needs to track usage of the courses and work with the vendor(s) to remove those that aren't "selling" (why pay for courses not being launched) and to keep the content fresh for frequent learners.

It is important to establish a sound e-learning infrastructure that enhances the quality of the learning experience and the confidence of an e-learner, who is likely to be anxious about this new approach to learning. As a result of building this firm foundation, you will have the opportunity to take advantage of e-learning options as technology and tools evolve. These issues can be intimidating, difficult, and unspectacular, but avoiding or shortcutting their resolution is likely to lead to problems in the future that will require much more effort, time, and resources—and may also impact your credibility. With this foundation in place, let's focus on what can be done to directly prepare the e-learner.

PREPARING THE E-LEARNER

The question of how to prepare and support learners for the new world of learning is important and intriguing. e-Learning has burgeoned onto the business learning landscape, and its unique opportunities and challenges demand that business learning professionals re-evaluate programs, rethink strategy, and retool skills. This is a multi-faceted challenge, requiring a multi-dimensional solution.

The Prudential Financial learning team recognizes that producing effective e-learning solutions that directly support the employees' work is perhaps the best way to get learners to enjoy this learning approach. We've observed that truly engaging and performance enhancing e-learning experiences have high relevance to the job. For e-learning, the closer to the job, the better.

For instance, an e-learning experience that describes the purpose of a particular task, provides a demonstration of how the procedure is done, and gives an opportunity to practice the procedure is a powerful learning experience. It is directly relevant to the work, builds on existing knowledge, enables the learner to see it applied, and allows the learner to practice in a fail-safe environment.

Preparing e-learners for this type of experience is not a challenge. For instance, Prudential Real Estate and Relocation Services (PRERS) recently consolidated five customer service locations spread across the United States into one international service operation in Phoenix, Arizona. The consolidation resulted in many experienced staff leaving the company and a large number of new employees being hired in Phoenix. Working with Integrated Performance Solutions and Harold Stolovitch and Associates, the business learning team at PRERS developed a blended learning solution and implemented it successfully.

The e-learning design was based on a simple "inform, show, and do" methodology. The e-learning components were designed in short, one-hour or less, modules. The modules were integrated with classroom instruction, facilitated performance sessions, structured-on-the-job experiences, e-role play simulations, and regular knowledge checks and assessments. Each e-learning module is designed to be multi-purposed, allowing new-to-position learners to use them in a sequential manner, while also serving as a performance support tool for the experienced performer who might need a quick refresher.

The outcome was a very successful transition. The business learning team was able to reduce the time required to achieve proficiency from a previous average of five months to six weeks, resulting in the formation of a well-trained six-hundred-person workforce in six months, three months ahead of schedule.

There does not appear to be a silver-bullet solution that will inspire every employee to seek the advantages of e-learning. Instead, a prudent approach of establishing modest expectations and focusing e-learning on the work appears to be more successful in the long term. Consider these approaches to successfully preparing e-learners.

Blending Is Best

We've developed the graphic in Figure 5.3 to help the Prudential Financial learning professionals explain blended learning:

Figure 5.3. Blended Learning Toolkit

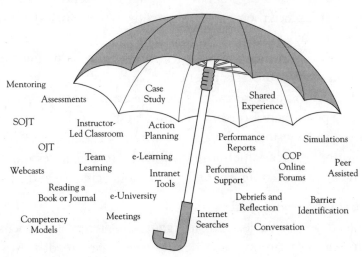

The graphic illustrates that there are many tools available to the business learning professional. They can be combined in many ways to improve the learning experience and the transfer of learning to performance. Our experience in Prudential Real Estate and Relocation Services, described earlier, illustrates the performance benefits of blending e-learning with other learning methodologies.

We have discovered some compelling data in support of blended learning. The Thomson Job Impact Study: The Next Generation of Corporate Learning showed that a blended learning technique delivered 30 percent higher performance improvement than did e-learning alone. In addition, the learning process was 30 percent faster using the blended approach. The study is available for free at www.netg.com/demosanddownloads.

Prepare the Leaders

Most business leaders value learning solutions that support their performance needs, but too often they feel that the learning solutions offered do not meet that standard. Business leaders are looking for a better approach to developing and maintaining the knowledge and skills of their workforce. Their goal is the same as ours. We are seeking learning tools that will shorten time to proficiency for new hires, provide just-in-time support for continuous performance improvement, reduce time away from the job, improve retention, help business leaders exceed their goals, and provide a means for a sustainable competitive advantage.

To deliver on the promise, e-learning requires a significant effort from many internal partners. We continually work with business leaders to illustrate and position e-learning as one aspect of a shift to a performance-oriented learning strategy. The business leaders need to be visible and vocal supporters of the new importance of learning. A successful transition will also require investments in technical infrastructure, talent, organizational change, and culture.

Modest e-Learning Goals

In transitioning to e-learning it is generally preferable to focus on quality rather than on speed, depth rather than breadth. At Prudential Financial we are taking a bulls-eye approach by initially establishing an objective of augmenting existing job-related courses with e-learning components so as to create a blended solution. Initially, we are hoping to motivate 20 percent to 25 percent of our employees to effectively and regularly use e-learning courses. In this way we hope to demonstrate the viability and ease of e-learning and gain support from business leaders and learners. We expect this pragmatic approach will enable us to gain momentum for acceptance and broader use of e-learning tools by most employees in support of our initiatives.

Resetting Expectations

To successfully establish e-learning in an organization, learner expectations must ultimately be validated and addressed. It is important to clearly define what the learning environment looks like and why it will support the learners' need to be successful. The learners should know:

- Product, service, and organizational changes will continue to drive learning needs.
- Self-directed learning is required to remain productive in an ever-changing environment.
- Most learning occurs within a few feet of their workplace.
- Learning is changing, from primarily a classroom instruction model to one that is more balanced, blending classroom with e-learning and other forms of learning activities.

CONCLUSION

Effectively preparing the e-learner is a systemic process. It requires a sound infrastructure, many technical and instructional standards, testing and quality assurance, blending, leadership support, and more. The learning professionals throughout Prudential Financial are continuously exploring new tools to enhance the learning experience and to increase the transfer of learning to performance.

One key lesson we've learned is to focus the e-learning activities on job-related tasks and processes. e-Learning is more effective when it directly supports the work. Our early experience utilizing this approach shows that it substantially reduces the challenge of preparing employees to use e-learning tools.

Organizational knowledge has never been more important to the success of an enterprise. As business learning professionals, our leaders look to us for the tools to enable employees to learn faster than the rate of change. We must learn to extend our comfort zones into the murkiness of e-learning to find the nuggets of goodness from which we will build better learning solutions, faster and less expensively.

Learning is the journey. Enjoy!

Reference

Brown, J.S., (2002, Feb.). Growingupdigital. *USDLA Journal*.

About the Author

Rick Rabideau, Ph.D., is the vice president of associate development for Prudential Financial. Rabideau's e-learning journey began as an instructor with Apple Computer, Inc., in the early 1980s, where he first merged his enthusiasm for learning with technology. He is a passionate advocate for advancing the business learning paradigm. He continuously searches for ideal tools to help employees enhance performance and, as a result, empower organizations with the most sustainable competitive advantage—knowledge.

Chapter 6

Organizational Best Practices for Preparing e-Learners

Jim Moshinskie

Comments from e-Learners

"I got lost at the start and never got found again."

"I don't see any advantage in it."

"It takes too long to learn what the software can and can't do."

AS E-LEARNING BECOMES MORE MAINSTREAM, best practices are slowly emerging to guide the implementation and administration of online courses. One such area is what organizations can do to prepare the learner for the e-learning experience. This chapter focuses on some of the best practices collected from e-LITE (e-Learning Incites Training Excellence), a weekly web-based training think tank that includes ten performance improvement technologists from both educational organizations and international corporations. E-LITE discussions have led to a number of white papers dealing with specific e-learning topics, such as blended learning, the use of learning objects, and e-learning evaluation. The best practices depicted below are a result of both the far-ranging conversations and the focused papers.

LINK TO THE LEARNERS' REAL NEEDS

One emerging message in today's information-rich e-learning environments is that employees must see how the training directly addresses their real needs in the workplace. Therefore, develop instructional objectives that demonstrate the usefulness of instruction matched with authentic exercises and concrete examples directly applicable to their daily struggles within the workplace. The course should contain goals with specific standards of performance that can be completed in a short time. It should match the learner's ability level and blatantly answer: "What's in it for me?"

BUILD STAKEHOLDER SUPPORT

Research shows that a supportive work environment motivates learners to transfer the new knowledge to the workplace (Broad, 1997). Successful organizations know that key stakeholders, such as managers, trainers, and peers, must closely participate in all phases of instructional design and then support the learners when the online training occurs. Managers and peers will be needed later to help fellow trainees avoid information overload anxiety by becoming active coaches and creating opportunities for practice and feedback by using collaborative technologies such as chat, voice chat, webcasts, and discussion threads. Let e-learners clearly see this support through promotions, newsletter articles, and emails.

MATCH THE
LEARNER'S VALUES AND MOTIVES

McClelland (1984) suggests that the notions of the need for power, achievement, or affiliation are powerful levers in explaining performance variations among individuals. While instruments to measure values, motives, and learning styles have existed for many years, they are not usually part of the assessment and design of face-to-face (F2F) learning events, let alone distance learning. In the case of web-based training, it may be critical that an understanding of the general value set mix of learners be established prior to design and delivery. These instruments can be found through organizations such as ASTD and publishers such as Jossey-Bass/Pfeiffer.

Both values and motives relate to behavior, but in different ways, as shown in Table 6.1. Values often influence people's choices about where to invest their energies, while motives reflect how much pleasure people get out of certain activities, such as being with people (high need for affiliation), doing better at challenging tasks (high need for achievement), or having impact or influence on others (high need for power). Table 6.2 presents some possible activities to engage learners' value orientations. While assessing the discrete mix of all learning groups may prove impractical, planning some activities that support different value orientations will increase the energy and enjoyment of the learner and may lead to greater completion rates.

Table 6.1. A Comparison of Value vs. Motives

Values	Motives
Choose areas of importance	Natural drives
Conscious level	Unconscious
Help an individual make decisions in current time	Predict types of behaviors a person will gravitate toward over time
Adaptive—developed from experiences throughout one's life	Basic—influenced by early emotional experiences and perhaps genetic
Less difficult to change	More difficult to change

Table 6.2. Matching Value and Motive
Attributes to Learner Motivation

Goal	Power	Achievement	Affiliation
Tapping into the Value Attribute	Believe that completing the learning event will make them more successful in influencing others.	Believe that the learning event will contribute to their success in the future.	See the learning group as referent. Should identify with other learners in the event.
Tapping into the Motive Attribute	May enjoy the learning more if they have the opportunity to direct or support the activities of others within the learning event.	May enjoy the learning more if they are given feedback on their progress in attaining goals during learning events.	May enjoy the learning more if they have the opportunity to work with others and develop increased rapport.

PREPARE THE WORK ENVIRONMENT

Make certain the workplace is prepared to support the completion of training and the application of new knowledge and skills. Tactics include simple housekeeping issues like making sure learners have web access and a quiet place to work. Ensure it is viewed as acceptable or safe to participate in training during working hours, if this is the case. Supervisors and managers should know the content to be covered (and ideally have completed the online course themselves). Train the supervisors on how to effectively coach and reinforce desired application of new knowledge and skills on the job. Surveys made on employees who participated in e-learning courses consistently show that their major complaint was the constant interruptions that interfered with their training. This particularly occurs when companies allow employees to take online courses at their workplace where customers, fellow employees, and phone calls can interrupt.

CONSIDER USING BOTH
PUSH AND PULL STRATEGIES

Push strategies are those that require and often monitor training completion. An advantage of the software programs used to manage e-learning (often referred to as a learning management system or LMS) is that they allow real-time tracking and reporting of training participation. Informing learners of this fact and having managers recognize early completers and alert laggards that their absence of participation is visible to management will often promote higher participation and completion rates. The principle here is to set an expectation and to "inspect what you expect."

Pull strategies, on the other hand, attempt to inspire rather than require the learner to complete the e-learning. Communication and promotion of the learning experience are among the most effective pull strategies. Remember, people will not complete training if they do not know it is available. You can find an excellent example of a successful pull strategy in Chapter 3.

Communications can take place through any medium or combination of media, for example, emails and newsletters. Conoco University distributed colorful mouse pads that advertised the course web address on them. David Weekly Homes of Houston issued miniature construction cones that could be placed on top of computer monitors that gave the URL for online courses and carried the slogan, "Mind Under Construction."

To be effective, your promotional literature should include one or more of these motivational strategies:

1. Focus on results—Tell learners what they will be able to accomplish by completing the e-learning. If possible, share success stories from alumni.

2. Focus on assuring success—Stress that the e-learning was designed around situations and needs of people like them, so it will be immediately applicable to them. Also, inform learners that the e-learning is structured so that successful completion

is well within their capabilities. Remember, fear of the unknown and fear of failure are significant barriers to training participation for many people. Consider sharing testimonials from other learners who had similar fears or doubts before they attempted the e-learning.

3. Enhance the importance of the learning process—Many learners are more motivated if they know a learning experience is endorsed by senior executives or recognized experts, is accredited or earns credit toward a degree or industry credentials, or earns tangible rewards, points, or other perks. Cover such facts in e-learning announcements.

4. Highlight the topics of interest—Even the most reluctant learners may be more motivated to participate in e-learning when they know a topic that interests them will be covered.

INCLUDE REWARDS

The non-instructional approaches can be of a monetary or non-monetary nature. Monetary compensation includes salary adjustments, perks, differential pay, time off with pay, or gifts. Non-monetary compensation includes improved working conditions, new tools and equipment, awards, and career opportunities (Thiagarajan, Estes, & Kemmerer, 1999).

If the effort will be tied to a certification system that clearly delineates to the workers what activities they need for advancement, motivation seems to increase. Other motivators to consider include admittance to a follow-up classroom event in a desired location such as a resort, maintenance of current certification, peer pressure, and peer recommendations, that is, respected peers speaking highly of the training.

PROVIDE A LEARNING PORTAL

The instructional team can create corporate-specific learning portals (that is, a page on the corporate intranet that serve as an entry point for the intended audience). Learning portals can be dynamically generated using a combination of employee profiles, pre-tests, and self-selection of topics of interest. The portal then presents to the employee a customized list of learning opportunities that are relevant to their level, responsibilities, and advancement goals— thereby increasing their motivation to take and complete courses specific to their developmental needs. These may include relevant company-offered courses, both classroom and distance learning, conferences, and university degree programs offered online, virtual discussion groups, virtual presentations, and online clipping services. This site should include not only the courses available, but also list any monetary and non-monetary awards as well.

EXAMINE METACOGNITIVE STRATEGIES

Learners bring their own interpretations of the virtual online environment and how they learn best from it. One way that performance technologists can better understand these interpretations is to pre-examine the metacognitive strategies used by learners during an online course. Metacognition addresses how a person learns, and it varies among people. After your learners finish a course, invite them "to think how they learn." Analyzing their reflections provides important metacognitive insight about their learning process. By collecting data on these processes, you can build an evolving database that can guide the development of future online learning events. For example, perhaps your target population does better in a synchronous environment rather than an asynchronous environment, or they may be more comfortable with simulations than with games (Campbell, Campbell, & Dickinson, 1996).

DETERMINE ENVIRONMENTAL FAVORABILITY

Motivation to transfer what was learned online to the actual workplace depends on trainees' perceptions of managerial and social support for the use of their new skills, referred to as *environmental favorability*. The learners can be asked several questions that specifically address their motivation to transfer using both open-ended and closed-end type responses (Machin & Fogarty, 1997). Once the data are collected from the trainees, appropriate statistical tools can analyze the data and perhaps uncover correlations to future performance.

Table 6.3 provides some open-ended questions that can yield information about both the motivation to transfer and metacognitive strategies used by your learners. Using the information, it will be possible to derive three ratings:

- Rating 1—The degree of motivation to see the course through to a successful end.
- Rating 2—The degree to which the person has effective strategies to be successful.
- Rating 3—The degree that each of the three primary driving levers of power, achievement, and affiliation motivate that particular student.

Table 6.3. Possible Questions to Measure Motivation

Why are you enrolled in this course?

What's in it for you if you are successful in this course?

How important is it to you to complete this course?

What does "success" mean to you with respect to this course?

Have you set objectives for yourself with respect to this course? If so, what are they?

What are the probabilities of you seeing this course through to its very end?

Do you foresee any challenges or difficulties that would get in the way or make it more difficult for you to complete this course?

Is there anything you know about how to learn that you will take into account in how you approach this course?

To what degree do you hope that this course will contribute to your ability to influence others more successfully in the work situations you face or are likely to face? (*power orientation*)

To what degree do you hope that this course will increase your ability to meet anticipated job challenges? (*achievement orientation*)

To what degree do you believe that working with others in the course is important to your learning? (*affiliation orientation*)

ALLOW TECHNICAL TEST SESSIONS

Many technical concerns can be overcome by simply allowing e-learners to practice using the interface before the course starts. During these test runs, have help desk personnel available to answer questions and solve technical problems immediately. Patience is the key. Webcasts are particularly vulnerable to delays when one participant interrupts progress with a technical problem that could have been solved before the session began.

CONCLUSION

In this chapter, I presented numerous strategies that can be used to prepare for a better e-learning experience. It is impossible and inadvisable to incorporate all these strategies in any one course. However, as you monitor and evaluate e-learning courses, you can determine which strategies work best for your particular target population. Thus, you can slowly move from creating online courses using intuition to having some theoretical basis for design and development. By monitoring the learner's responses to these techniques and developing a metacognitive approach unique to your audience, you can increase the effectiveness of online learning and make it a more effective tool in our performance improvement toolbox.

References

Broad, M. (1997). Overview of transfer of training: From learning to performance. *Performance Improvement Quarterly, 10*(2), 7–21.

Campbell, L., Campbell, B., & Dickinson, D. (1996). *Teaching and learning through multiple intelligences.* Needham Heights, MA: Simon & Schuster.

Machin, M., & Fogarty, G. (1997). The effects of self-efficacy, motivation to transfer, and situational constraints on transfer intentions and transfer of training. *Performance Improvement Quarterly, 10*(2), 98–115.

McClelland, D. (1984). *Human motivation.* Cambridge, MA: Cambridge Press.

Thiagarajan, S., Estes, F., & Kemmerer, F. (1999). Designing compensation systems to motivate performance improvement. In H. Stolovitch & E. Keeps (Eds.), *Handbook of human performance technology* (2nd ed.), (pp. 411–429). San Francisco: Jossey-Bass.

About the Author

Dr. Jim Moshinskie serves as the Accenture Professor of Human Performance at Baylor University, Waco, Texas. Dr. Mo, as he is better known, coordinates the new performance improvement technologies major in the Hankamer School of Business and directs the Center for Corporate E-Learning. The Center conducts e-learning pilots and sponsors one-day boot camps onsite to corporate trainers entitled E-Learning Made E-Z. Dr. Mo enjoys converting content into interactive e-learning, and his efforts have led to his winning ISPI Awards of Excellence for Instructional Interventions in 2000 and 2001. He can be reached at James_Moshinskie@baylor.edu.

This chapter was produced with the e-LITE (e-Learning Incites Training Excellence) Think Tank. Members include Claude Balthazard, Ph.D., Organizational Studies, Inc.; Larry Carille, Ph.D., A.T. Kearney, Inc.; Chris Good, Motorola University; Ira Kasdan, Performance Leaders; William N. Knapp, Deloitte Consulting, chair; Ara Ohanian, VuePoint Corporation; Bruno Strasser, Werner-Siemens-Schule Training Center, Stuttgart, Germany; Michael Van-Hoozer, Accenture; Michael Walsh, SynerProject; and John Boyd, VuePoint Corporation.

Chapter 7

Preparing and Supporting e-Learners

The Organizational Change Imperative

Ronnie Kurchner-Hawkins

Comments from e-Learners

"I get confused in the technical terminology from the start. Can't they use words to describe what the stuff is that isn't 'computerese'?"

"You only get out of it what you put into it."

> "Organizations that do not modify themselves to absorb newly adopted technologies never achieve their technological promise."
>
> *Davis, 1986, p. 1*

E-LEARNING HAS BEEN EMBRACED by business and industry—its acceptance and growth are clear. Estimates of the spending on e-learning by the year 2004 run as high as $14 billion. e-Learning is not just e-training. It is bringing information, knowledge, and expertise to the learner using electronic (e) tools. Although these tools have allowed us to expand the possibilities for learning, and we hope the probability of learning, they do not guarantee it. As we learned years ago, having technology does not guarantee its successful use in organizations. Unfortunately for many organizations that have been quick to jump at e-learning as one viable route for building workforce competence, they have learned the lesson that *just because you build it—doesn't mean the learners will come or, for that matter, stay.* Organizations will need to focus on how to change in order to accommodate and capitalize on e-learning. The stakes are too high for organizations not to effectively prepare and support e-learners.

Here is an all too familiar scenario being played out in many companies. Although the scenario is fiction, the issues and problems this scenario represents are real to many companies.

> The vice president of human resources was sold on moving to e-learning solutions. She understood the potential benefits to her company of availability 24/7, just-in-time learning, and high ROI. She could see the financial and logistical advantages, since the e-learning initiative could be scaled up and provided globally without substantial cost. It seemed appropriate to use e-learning for her company's new technology initiative, since the cost for classroom-based training was going to be considerable and difficult to implement in a short timeframe. e-Learning tools would be used to train employees worldwide about the new technology. She contacted a number of vendors and asked them to provide an estimate of what it would cost to convert some of the technical training to web-based programs.
>
> Due diligence, including a training needs analysis, was done to be sure that the content was appropriate for the target group and the training platform was user-friendly. The courses created were well-designed and engaging.
>
> When the program was rolled out, there were problems accessing technical support, servers were overloaded, bandwidth differences affected the ability to view some content, and some participants had difficulty logging on to the program. Some participants were frustrated when they couldn't find and complete the final assessment. The completion rates were extremely low, and the majority of the target group never even went to the intranet site to look at the programs.

The vice president of HR and her team learned that there is much more to integrating e-learning into an organization than excellent design and development of the programs.

What went wrong? Successfully implementing e-learning requires focusing on how to create and support change in the organization. A useful theoretical approach for understanding how change occurs in organizations is the *diffusion of innovation* framework. If we approach e-learning as an innovation and preparing and supporting of e-learners as part of the "change process," there are a number of insights and courses of action that become apparent. We can determine how to support and prepare e-learners by paying close attention to four key elements of this framework. The elements are

1. The Diffusion of Innovation Model;
2. Innovation characteristics;
3. The innovation-decision process; and
4. Adopter characteristics.

This chapter will present these key elements and how they can be applied for integrating e-learning in organizations. The focus will be on how to prepare and support e-learners. Examples will be drawn from companies that have confronted many of these implementation issues.

THE DIFFUSION OF INNOVATION MODEL

The diffusion of innovation is both an individual and a social process. Diffusion is the process by which an innovation is communicated through particular channels over time among the members of a social system (Rogers, 1995).

**Figure 7.1. Diffusion, the Process by Which
(1) an Innovation Is (2) Communicated Through
Certain Channels (3) over Time (4) Among
the Members of a Social System**

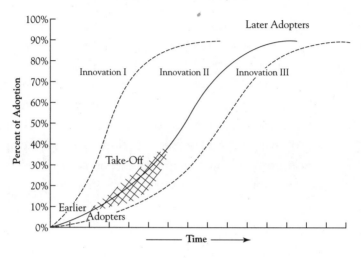

Rogers, 1995, p. 11.

An innovation is an idea, practice, or object that an individual or other unit of adoption (for example, an organization or department) perceives as new. The channels used to communicate the innovation can be mediated (for example, mass media) or interpersonal. Time is how long it takes until the innovation is adopted throughout the social system. The social system that we are usually concerned with for e-learning adoption and use is the organization. Generally this rate of adoption is represented by the "S" curve in Figure 7.1. Notice that for each innovation there is a slower start with a quick ramp up and then a subsequent slowing down in system-wide use as the innovation permeates the system or an improved innovation picks up where the other left off. Research in this field suggests that the acceptance, adoption, and use of innovations can be influenced by characteristics of the innovation and the adopter's perceptions (Rogers, 1995). This implies that how an e-learner (adopter) perceives the e-learning (innovation) experience will influence its use or disuse. We can also view e-learning as an umbrella term for a number of innovations. For example, asynchronous, self-paced learning modules are one type of innovation. Synchronous webcasts and blended learning programs that combine virtual classroom experiences with chat rooms and coaches are others. We could even approach each rollout of a new program as an innovation. Therefore, we should not assume that e-learning A = e-learning B = e-learning C in the perception of our target audiences.

Innovation Characteristics and e-Learning Decision Making

There are five characteristics of innovations: (1) relative advantage, (2) compatibility, (3) complexity, (4) trialability, and (5) observability. Rate of adoption is determined by how these characteristics are perceived by potential users (Rogers, 1995). This implies that the decision to use or stop using an innovation is "in the mind of the beholder." Innovations that are perceived by individuals as having greater relative advantage, compatibility, trialability, observability, and *less* complexity will be adopted more rapidly than other innovations (Roger, 1995). Let's explore how each of these concepts can be applied to e-learners' decision-making process.

1. Relative Advantage

Relative advantage is how much better the potential user perceives the current innovation to be than the one that preceded it. The degree of relative advantage may be economic; however, social prestige, convenience, and satisfaction are also important factors. Relative advantage is a subjective measure (Rogers, 1995). In the case of e-learning, if the learners perceive e-learning as better than other approaches, they are more likely to use it initially and continue to use it. Additionally, if they link the e-learning to business objectives and/or people or groups with revenue stream, prestige, or credibility, then the chances of using the programs are even greater.

During the early days of e-learning at Dell Computer, Michael Dell promoted and championed e-learning courses. He regularly took the online classes and let people know, via the company intranet, how important learning was for the company. Employees wanted to be "like Michael." Michael Dell's picture was used on certificates of completion that were distributed after completion of the online courses. Employees displayed the certificates proudly in their workspaces. People noticed and commented on who had the certificates. The prevailing culture clearly promoted online learning.

A major selling point for e-learning has always been that learners have access anywhere and anytime. Convenience for the learner is an advantage that is a cornerstone of e-learning's appeal.

A large financial services company instituted e-learning programs for its salesforce in response to concerns that training took them away from their clients. Participants' program evaluations identified convenience as one of the things they liked best about the program.

The key to supporting e-learners is to maintain user satisfaction, make it as convenient to use as possible, and build a social structure that supports continuation. Confirming and reinforcing relative advantage may encourage continued use of e-learning and/or e-learning programs and reduce dropouts (disuse).

2. Compatibility

Compatibility is how consistent the innovation is with the existing values, past experiences, culture, and the needs of users. If an innovation is incompatible with the prevailing culture, it will not be adopted as rapidly as one that is compatible. If an organization does not perceive e-learning or learning in general as important in the organization, it may take longer for e-learning to be used. Part of the change process will need to focus on building positive experiences with learning and e-learning and linking e-learning to users' needs.

At a financial services company whose prevailing culture focused on pushing sales goals to the highest limit, the intranet home page advertised the career and financial benefits of taking the e-learning program. The home page provided a direct link to the program. The concept of "produce or out" was taken seriously by all employees. Linking e-learning to sales goals resulted in more employees exploring and taking the program.

The adoption of an incompatible innovation often requires major changes to the value system/culture, which is a relatively slow process. For example, if there is a perceived value that learning must occur in a classroom, or prior experiences with e-learning were frustrating, then there is a lower probability that someone will use an e-learning solution. In this case, blended learning experiences may provide learners with a level of comfort that allows them to ease into e-learning and obtain the support they need.

After focusing attention on the development of a series of online learning courses, one Fortune 100 company learned that the reason their employees were not completing online programs was a high number of interruptions. Because people were sitting at their own desks while in training, other employees assumed that they were available to conduct business. Eventually, employees used signs to indicate when they were participating in an online course and not to be disturbed. In some cases, employees left their desks and went to a "learning area" to take the online program. The rate of course completion increased considerably.

Compatibility also raises issues about learning styles and learning needs of e-learners. A one-size-fits-all model of supporting e-learners will probably not work.

An executive leadership forum at a large global computer company provided both face-to-face time for executives to problem solve and an ongoing online forum for continued discussions around strategic leadership issues. The executives wanted the flexibility to use the group as a sounding board around issues and participate when possible given their packed schedules.

We may need to provide a range of support mechanisms such as help tools, telephone support, chat rooms, or coaches who are compatible with a range of learning styles and accept the fact that for some individuals it will be more difficult using e-learning.

3. Complexity

Complexity is the degree to which it is difficult to understand and use the innovation. Innovations that are simpler to understand and use are adopted more rapidly. Innovations that require the adopter to develop new skills and knowledge will take longer to be adopted. This is an important concept as we determine how and when to support and prepare e-learners. If learners feel that e-learning is more difficult, they will be reluctant to try it. The time it takes for people to successfully use e-learning may also be affected by perceptions of the complexity of the technology.

The more complex the e-learning experience, the more support we must provide so that learners feel comfortable and continue to use e-learning. Coaches, technical support, feedback, and help systems may need to be embedded in the e-learning systems. For example, Cisco Systems had to rethink supporting employees' use of web-based tools and the complexity of the tools when performance problems became apparent.

> Cisco Systems, a recognized leader in implementing web-based applications, identified a problem with the implementation of its virtual manufacturing processes. Employees' incorrect use of web-based tools caused major problems. To address this issue, Cisco developed training, used expert coaches, certified users, and targeted user needs and knowledge levels. Once the additional training allowed people to become proficient, they "eagerly adopted" the web-based tools. As

a result of the program, Cisco changed how it prepared and supported those employees who must use the tools. Now Cisco provides new employees with training on how to use the web-based tools and ongoing support in online training modules that double as a user guide. Coaches, subject-matter experts, and IT staff are still available to users (www.Cisco.com).

4. Trialability

Trialability is the degree to which users can try out or experiment with using the innovation. New ideas that can be tried in small doses will generally be adopted more quickly. It reduces the risk to the user. Trialability of e-learning can take a variety of forms—from orienting practice sessions to mini-modules. We need to get people to the "e-learning table" so they can have a taste of the experience.

> Prior to launching a series of web-based, self-paced programs, one company began a marketing campaign that allowed users to access some modules. These modules provided them with useful information that they could apply immediately.

The trial needs to be a positive experience or it is unlikely that e-learning will be readily incorporated into the employee's approach to learning and performance improvement. Providing a safe venue for e-learners to experience an e-learning program, learning how to use the software and hardware prior to rolling out the program, can support continued use.

> Before attending a web-based symposium, participants had the opportunity to review the basics of participating in the program. They received an explanation of the icons, procedures for interacting with the speakers and other participants, and a simulation of the experience.

This approach not only encouraged people to take the programs, but it also provided a means for trying out the program and experiencing its benefits.

5. Observability

Observability is the degree to which the impact of the innovation is immediately observable. The easier it is for individuals to see the results of an innovation, the more likely they are to adopt it. Any time we can create an opportunity for learning where it can quickly be applied and used successfully, we increase the probability that it will be used. There is another benefit to observability. Observability may stimulate interpersonal networks. Information can spread quickly through these networks. The visibility of an innovation encourages peer discussion about what the innovation is like.

> A new employee orientation program was launched on a fast-growing technology company's intranet. All employees were encouraged to go to the site to "check it out" at a company-wide meeting. Only after a number of new employees commented on how useful the site was to their coworkers did these employees go to the site.

If people discuss positive experiences, they sell the innovation to others through their communication. It's the "buzz" created when people are talking about "a good thing." Inside an organization, creating a positive view of e-learning will get more people to use it. It can also get them to persist in trying e-learning, even if it is complex and difficult to use. The reverse also may be true. Negative e-learning experiences, when observed and communicated in the organization, may create an obstacle to people using e-learning.

E-learning that is perceived as having *greater* relative advantage, compatibility, trialability, observability, and *less* complexity will be used more readily. A misconception that has unfortunately surprised e-learning champions and implementers is the belief that making e-learning simple, easy to use, and readily accessible is enough. If other factors such as relative advantage and compatibility are at odds with using e-learning, then there will still be difficulties in getting the initiative in place. We need to consider all of these innovation characteristics as we determine how to support and prepare e-learners in our organizations.

The Innovation-Decision Process: Preparing and Supporting e-Learners

The innovation-decision process also provides clues on how to support and prepare e-learners. If our goal is to prepare and support e-learners successfully, we need to target the appropriate communication throughout the process. The innovation-decision process provides insight into both the communication and information we need to provide potential e-learners and when we need to target our communication and support.

The innovation-decision process is described as occurring in the following sequential stages:

1. Knowledge,
2. Persuasion,
3. Decision,
4. Implementation, and
5. Confirmation.

We know that, in some cases, individuals do not make the decision to use an innovation. A decision is made for them. In these cases, the knowledge and persuasion stages may follow the decision stage.

1. Knowledge
This stage occurs when an individual is exposed to the existence of the innovation and learns about how it functions. Two types of knowledge are needed: "how to" and the "principles" knowledge. Much of our support and preparation of e-learners focuses on providing these types of knowledge.

"*How to*" knowledge consists of information necessary to be able to use the innovation correctly. In the case of e-learning, it might be how to navigate learning online, what to do when confronted with a technical problem, how to participate in a "break out" room, raise your hand in a class, or even what number to call for expert assistance. It could be as simple as "how to log on" to the intranet site.

> A technology company spent considerable time and effort designing a blended learning solution for orienting new employees. It launched the program and then, to the dismay of the HR department, there were very few users of the new employee website in spite of emails encouraging visits to the site. It was quickly determined that there had been no directions provided in the emails about how to access the site and where to locate the employee's password.

> One company decided to speed up the new employee orientation process by creating online modules about how to use the company intranet. Even though most new employees were technology savvy, it did not follow that they would know how to productively use the company's intranet resources. Providing this "how to" information greatly reduced employee assimilation time.

"How to" knowledge helps the e-learner know what to do and reduces the individual's sense of uncertainty and discomfort. Learning guides and classroom preparation for e-learning provide this "how to" knowledge. The amount of "how to" knowledge needed for proper use is much greater for complex innovations than for those that are less complex. If an adequate level of "how to" knowledge is not obtained prior to trial and adoption of the innovation, rejection, or discontinuance is likely to result (Rogers, 1995). This may explain some of the high dropout rates for e-learning programs.

Principles-knowledge deals with the functioning principle underlying how the innovation works. Understanding the underlying principles of e-learning may be essential for ensuring it is used correctly. It is possible to adopt and use an innovation without possession of principles knowledge, but the long-range competence of individuals to assess future innovations (successive e-learning experiences) is facilitated by principles know-how (Rogers, 1995).

Without this type of knowledge, learners may not use features of the e-learning experience and aspects of the learning experience may be lost.

A large financial services company decided to transition compo-nents of its year-long branch managers' training from classroom-based to self-paced online learning. The cost savings from reduced travel expenses, time away from the office, and reduction of the printing and distribution costs of regularly updating the materials were important motivations to make the change. The online pro-gram consisted of self-paced modules with an embedded simulation that learners would complete between classroom sessions. During the launch of the program, the corporate office received a number of requests from participants for hard copies of all the online materials. It was clear that the underlying principles of e-learning were not ap-parent to these participants. To address this apparent resistance to using the technology, the vice president of retail services attended a number of the sessions and openly talked about the benefits of using the online programs. Two of the benefits discussed were a reduction in printing and paper costs and the ability to change the content of the online programs to conform to changing policies and proce-dures. Also, a group of highly respected executives served as mentors to the branch managers and reiterated the rationale and benefits of the online learning program to the participants. They discussed the underlying principles of e-learning and reiterated the financial in-centives for participating in all aspect of the program. Additional "how to" support was provided to the participants so they could eas-ily use the online simulation and materials.

e-Learning technology is constantly changing. This may affect both the quality of the learning design and the learners' experi-ence. Learners who understand the underlying principles of how to learn using mediated (electronic) resources may become more adaptable to the technology changes as they occur. For example, learners who have experienced assessments online may be more

amenable to embedded questioning that could be part of sophisti-
cated branching programs. These e-learners can eventually take a
more active role in determining the mode and method of learning.
Both "how to" and the "principles" type knowledge may be needed
for preparing and supporting e-learners.

2. Persuasion

This stage occurs when an individual forms a favorable or unfa-
vorable opinion. The types of communication people receive can
influence their decision to use the innovation. This stage may require answers to questions such as "What are the consequences to
me if I use this innovation?" "What advantages or disadvantages
are there for doing this?" "How will it affect my well-being and future?" Research has found that answers to these questions provided
by respected peers are more likely to get the individual to adopt the
innovation (Rogers, 1995).

> To launch a new online program, a Fortune 100 company advertised
> it on the intranet home page, displayed posters in the cafeteria and
> throughout buildings, and sent emails to the targeted audience ex-
> tolling the benefits of participating in the program. Participants who
> completed the program were entered into a lottery for a prize. After
> the initial programs, participant testimonials encouraged others to
> take the program.

3. Decision

This stage occurs when an individual engages in activities that lead
to a choice to use or not use the innovation. The degree to which
others are actively engaged in e-learning may influence use. The social aspect of this process can come into play as in the case with e-
learning at Dell. At Dell, the prevailing culture provided a strong
pull toward accepting and using e-learning. In some instances, the
only way Dell employees could acquire certain types of training was
through the intranet site. There was an expectation that learning
could and should occur anywhere and any time and that employees
would take advantage of the programs offered.

4. Implementation

This stage occurs when an individual puts the innovation into use on a regular basis. There is behavioral change. The continued support provided by "how-to" and "principles type" knowledge is essential. There is still a level of uncertainty about the benefits and outcomes from using the innovation. The user requires both technical support and reassurance to motivate the person to continue implementation.

> Building on a series of classroom-based executive programs on strategic business issues, a Fortune 100 company created an online learning network to encourage ongoing information exchange and peer learning. A facilitator, assigned to the network, encouraged exchange, raised issues, provided technical support, and maintained the database in a useful form. The facilitator maintained regular contact with all the participants to assure that the network continued to meet their needs.

5. Confirmation

This stage occurs when an individual seeks reinforcement of the decision to use or not use the innovation, at which point either continued use or disuse occurs. If the individual receives conflicting messages about the innovation, then a change in behavior may occur.

Preparing and supporting e-learners does not stop once a decision is made to use e-learning. The e-learners may experience considerable pressures that affect their continued use of e-learning. Karen Frankola, former e-learning solutions manager for NYUonline and currently an e-learning consultant, identified a number of reasons for high e-learner dropout rates:

- Learners don't have enough time;
- Lack of management oversight;
- Lack of motivation;
- Problems with technology;
- Lack of student support—technical, administrative, and academic;

- Individual learning preferences;
- Poorly designed courses; and
- Substandard and/or inexperienced instructors.

Many of these issues can and should be addressed through preparation and support. We cannot assume once an e-learning decision is made that it won't change. Supporting e-learners as they confront their choice is crucial.

ADOPTER CHARACTERISTICS: WHAT ARE E-LEARNERS LIKE?

"Depending on the employee group, some will be more receptive to online learning and technology, others will require a longer learning curve."

www.Cisco.com

e-Learners do not approach the e-learning experience equally. As Everett Rogers (1995) so aptly points out, "Individual innovation-decisions are idiosyncratic and particularistic" (p. 111). One of the key predictors of receptivity to an innovation is an individual's level of innovativeness, the degree to which someone is early to use and adopt innovations. There are five idealized adopter categories that members of a social system can be partitioned into on the basis on their innovativeness: (1) innovators, (2) early adopters, (3) early majority, (4) late majority, and (5) laggards, as shown in Table 7.1.

As you can see from the table, adopters, identified by when they decide to use an innovation, have different characteristics. e-Learners who are innovators may require and prefer different types of support and knowledge than laggards. As we design our support strategy, the more we know about the e-learner, the easier it may be to address knowledge and skill gaps as we support them. For example, learners (innovators) who volunteer to be the first to try a new program of

Table 7.1. Characteristics of Adopters

	Innovators	Early Adopters	Early Majority	Late Majority	Laggards
Order of Adoption of an Innovation	1	2	3	4	5
Percent of the Population	2.5%	13.5%	34%	34%	16%
Characteristics	• Focused on new ideas • Communication outside local circles • Belongs to cliques of innovators • Able to cope with high uncertainty • Brings new ideas into system • May not be respected or an opinion leader	• Integrated into the local system • Respected by peers • Tends to be an opinion leader • Role model • Provides subjective evaluation of innovations to near peers through interpersonal networks	• Adopts new ideas just before the majority • A third of the members of the system • Interacts frequently with peers • Shows willingness to innovate but seldom leads	• Adopts new ideas after the average member of the local system • A third of the members of the system • Skeptical and cautious about innovations • Peer pressure motivates adoption • Must feel certain that adopting the innovation is safe	• Last to adopt the innovation • Not opinion leaders • Focus is local • Many are isolated in the social system • Reference point is the past • Suspicious of innovation and change • May be financial reasons for not readily accepting an innovation

Adopted from Rogers, 1995.

e-learning tools may be more willing to deal with technical problems. They may be intrigued by how and why the e-learning programs work, while learners (late majority) who wait to make sure "all the bugs are ironed out of the program" may be less tolerant of technical problems and more apt to drop out as soon as they confront any problems using the e-learning tools.

Understanding e-learner characteristics, such as learning styles or psychological profiles, may eventually lead to tailored e-learning experiences. Technological advances in the future might support individualized content and media (for example, "intelligent e-tutors" or personalized 3D simulations). Currently, creating e-learning to reflect the learning styles, psychological profiles, and preferences of the e-learners would be cost-prohibitive and difficult to justify. At this point in the evolution of e-learning technology, content often determines the medium. Most e-learning is generally one-size-fits-all. The program is designed and the learner has limited choices as to how to get at the content. We should however, use our knowledge of e-learner characteristics, with our knowledge of the gaps between what e-learners prefer or need and the e-learning they will experience, to determine the type, level, and kind of support and preparation to provide.

BUILDING AN ORGANIZATIONAL CHANGE STRATEGY FOR PREPARING AND SUPPORTING E-LEARNERS

"Our primary driver for implementing e-learning is to get out of the way of people learning. We wanted to avoid churning people through classroom training and make training more available."

Towers Perrin's chief learning officer
in Computerworld, *July 16, 2001.*

It is clear from a change management perspective that a laissez-faire approach that assumes technology will take care of learning doesn't work. Learning requires the engagement of the learner in the process.

Our approach must not just be supportive but active. As we have learned from the Diffusion of Innovation Framework, using e-learning as a means for getting out of the way of people learning is about:

- Encouraging and developing the need for changing learning in the organization;
- Removing and overcoming obstacles to e-learning that are inherent in the innovation (e-learning), the change process, the learner, and the system;
- Building and sustaining environments conducive to e-learning; and
- Encouraging and supporting the use of e-learning.

As we build our strategy for preparing and supporting e-learners, we need to assess both:

- Our learners' capacity and capabilities and
- Our organization's capacity to foster and support the e-learning initiative.

This approach will help us determine the gap between where we are currently and where we want to be and then what we will need to do. The chart in Figure 7.2 identifies three areas and the types of questions we will need to answer as we plan our strategy for preparing and supporting e-learners.

Figure 7.2. Strategy Planning Questions for Preparing and Supporting e-Learners

Learners

How is e-learning perceived—advantages, risks?

How computer literate are they?

How literate are they?

How technology savvy?

Figure 7.2. Strategy Planning Questions for Preparing and Supporting e-Learners, Cont'd

How receptive to e-learning?

Do they perceive e-learning as advantageous?

Are they self-directed?

Do they prefer learning via interaction?

How do they learn? Learning styles?

Is there fear of assessment or that others know what they can or cannot do?

Do they need to touch those who convey expert information?

How comfortable with learning technology and tools?

Are learners given time to learn—when, where, and how?

Is learning a priority?

Culture

What is the culture of learning and innovation? Is learning a priority?

What is the support for learning? Key decision makers? Managers? Peers?

Are there incentives for learning?

Are employee development and growth rewarded?

Is there a culture of independence and self-sufficiency?

Will independent learning mesh with how people view their jobs and work?

What is the history of flexibility in response to change?

Does management support e-learning?

Is learning viewed as strategically linked to business success?

Technology

What is the access to technology?

What is the ability to use technology?

What is the technology capacity and capability?

What are the IT support systems? Help systems?

What is the experience with technology failure?

This is by no means an exhaustive list. It may, however, help us to start to ask questions that will have to be answered as we build our e-learning change strategy. The ultimate goals of any e-learning endeavor within an organization are performance and results. To achieve these goals, organizations must look beyond the e-learning technology as the whole solution and focus on how people and the organization are key ingredients in the successful transition to e-learning.

References

Cisco Systems. *e-learning for manufacturing*. www.cisco.com/warp/public/10/wwtraining/elearning/educate/cases/manufacturing.pdf

Davis, D. D. (1986). *Managing technological innovation*. San Francisco: Jossey-Bass.

Frankola, K. e-Learning taboo—High dropout rates: Best practices for increasing online course completion rates, www.nyuonline.com/vn_3/inside/articles/learning_taboo.html

Rogers, E.M. (1995). *Diffusion of innovations* (4th ed.). New York: The Free Press.

About the Author

Ronnie H. Kurchner-Hawkins is president of Kurchner-Hawkins Associates, a small custom organizational research, design, development, and training company that provides consulting services for productivity improvement. She has worked with a broad cross section of private and public sector organizations. She has authored and co-authored many papers and reports on organizational issues and presented at national and international conferences on topics including e-learning, organizational assessment, change, leading virtually, and new employee assimilation. She received her Ph.D. from Michigan State University in organizational communication with an emphasis on organizational networks, organizational change, and labor and industrial relations. She can be reached at kurchnerhawkins@compuserve.com.

Chapter 8

The Roles of the Learner and the Instructor in e-Learning

George Siemens and Stephen Yurkiw

Comments from e-Learners

"When I first started, I needed someone to show me how, and then leave me alone."

"The instructor should have explained how the software worked."

ONE OF TWO MISTAKES is commonly made by organizations that embrace e-learning: They think e-learning is exactly the same as regular learning or they think e-learning is completely different from regular learning. While neither of these extreme views is accurate, at its heart, e-learning is a *different* way to learn. It is about a new interface between student and content. It is about rethinking the role of the instructor—a guide or a sage? As such, the process, the experience, the interface, the roles of student and instructor, all differ from traditional classrooms.

What is similar? The cyber student is still the same as the classroom student. The same principles of motivation apply, the same need for variety is there, and the same need for connectivity with the instructor and with other students exists. Students in a classroom or online are students first—the attachment of *classroom* or *online* refers not to the student, but to the medium through which a student will interact with the content. It is important, therefore, to consider that online learning is about learning, not about technology. The role of technology is to serve the learning process, not dominate it.

Failure to recognize the unique process of online learning, or the similarity of classroom and online students, has the potential to derail e-learning in an organization. It is important for organizations to understand the dynamics of e-learning and focus on implementing a strategy to prepare e-learners for the experience. The promises of e-learning are negated when organizations fail: (1) to prepare learners for how to e-learn or (2) to prepare instructors in how to facilitate e-learning.

THE ROLE OF TECHNOLOGY

Before exploring the roles of learner and instructor, it is necessary to form a proper view of the role of technology in learning. Technology enables more effective learning when properly utilized. Student success in learning online can be greatly enhanced when a variety of tools are used. Chat, whiteboards, discussion questions, synchronous instruction, voice over IP, file swapping, and so on all contribute to the creation of a rich learning environment, if used appropriately. As in a regular classroom, however, misuse of teaching aids results in ineffective learning. A learning tool should be evaluated in light of the intended learning objectives. For example, if a learning objective is to challenge a student's ability to think through course material, it may be appropriate to use a tool like threaded discussions, where students have time to evaluate and reflect on the material. If interaction and thinking "on your feet" were being evaluated, a chat tool would be more effective. Whatever the objective, the tool selected must match desired learning outcomes.

An instructor should use technology as a means of connecting with students, not a means of overwhelming them. A strategy that we use with our courses is to present various tools to new students gradually as the course progresses. For example, the first few weeks of instruction might only use threaded discussions. The third week might require using chat, then whiteboard, voice over IP, and so forth. This approach allows both the students and the instructor to orient to new technology, rather than being overwhelmed by it.

THE ROLE OF THE STUDENT IN SUCCESSFUL e-LEARNING

The starting point for student success is to involve the student in clarifying his or her assumptions about what it means to learn online. First-time students have a variety of views on online learning: "It should be easy," "It's a joke," "Online learning is second-rate to classroom learning," "Online learning is the same as classroom learning," and so on. Students need to understand their own views of online learning.

This exposure is simply metacognition—getting the student to think about his or her thinking of online learning. The more accurately a student's assumptions match the reality of an online experience, the greater the likelihood for success. For example, the student who feels online courses are easy may find that a self-test challenges those assumptions, resulting in a shift in perspective of what it means to be an online learner.

Self-Awareness

We designed a series of questions that lead students to evaluate their assumptions of online learning. Often, this evaluation challenges perceptions sufficiently to align a student's belief with the reality of e-learning. Table 8.1 lists questions used and the values assigned to each question.

Table 8.1. Questions and Values

Question	Scoring
Are you self-motivated when learning new skills?	Yes = 1
Are you a self-disciplined person?	Yes = 1
Do you set goals for yourself?	Yes = 1
Do you procrastinate in completing assignments and studying for tests?	No = 1
Are you comfortable with chat or instant messenger programs?	Yes = 1
Are you comfortable with email?	Yes = 1
Do you tend to participate in class discussions?	Yes = 1
In your regular courses, do you find that you end up "cramming" in order to complete assignments on time or to study for exams?	No = 1
Do you learn from your fellow students sharing their experiences?	Yes = 1
An instructor should be the expert, providing all the answers.	No = 1
I like to work independently.	Yes = 1
I enjoy technology, surfing the Internet, and exploring new information.	Yes = 1
I rely on my instructor to remind me of tests and assignment due dates.	No = 1
I enjoy learning on my own, at my own pace.	Yes = 1
I like to figure things out on my own.	Yes = 1
I like to participate in group work assignments.	Yes = 1
I like trying new skills and technology. I'm excited about the prospect of taking a course online.	Yes = 1
I believe online courses are an effective way to learn.	Yes = 1

Table 8.1. Questions and Values, Cont'd

Score	Online Learning Readiness
14 to 18	You are highly motivated and possess the skills needed to succeed at online learning. You will find that online learning allows you to utilize your organizational and planning skills. Enjoy!
7 to 13	You should do well in an online learning environment. Motivation, organization, and planning are the most critical aspects of succeeding online. If you keep current with course materials and follow the assignment submission schedule, you should do well in this online course.
1 to 6	Online learning may not suit your skills and approach to learning. This, however, does not mean that you will not be a good student. It means that you will have to be focused and committed to completing material on time.

The self-test serves primarily to help a student to think about his or her assumptions. Many students have commented on the value of the self-test in raising their awareness of some of the dynamics of learning online. Some of the values assigned may change based on the course. A course that has little discussion would alter a self-test to reflect the uniqueness of that course.

Our biased view is that all students can learn to succeed online. This view is reflected in that we do not attempt to use the self-test as a tool for students to "de-select" themselves as online students. Even students who scored poorly in preparedness to embrace online learning were instructed to focus instead on the areas that could be improved in order to enhance the prospect for success. Students who scored low in the self-test are encouraged to create a study plan that addresses some of their weaknesses. In cases where a student is not familiar with technology or software, he or she can be directed to remedial resources.

The self-test is simply a tool used to awaken students to the uniqueness of learning online. Additional student preparation activities include: detailed course schedule, tutorials on new software, preparation of a study plan to address individual "weaknesses" of learning online, and email/chat/discussion contact with each student immediately after the course begins. All of these activities are geared to aligning the student's perceptions and expectations with the reality of the online experience.

After students have been exposed to the dynamics of e-learning through the self-test, have completed basic software tutorials, have prepared a personal study plan, and have experienced cyber contact with the instructor, they should then be asked to follow guidelines of the course schedule. Regular, weekly activities need to be scheduled to ensure that students do not fall behind. These activities may include short reflective journals (one to two hundred words), contributions to discussion threads, synchronous chat sessions, or scheduled "virtual meetings" with the instructor.

Orientation to Online

Once a student has been oriented to the online environment and is comfortable navigating content and using communication tools, he or she can then begin to get involved in learning. Content learning, however, will not happen while the student is learning about the process of learning online or is still being oriented to the course software.

Students need to progress through several layers of orientation before they are at a point where learning will be maximized. These levels of orientation are

- *The computer.* This is the first level of orientation for learners new to computers. Basic skills needed at this level are starting the computer, using the operating system, and using various components (printer, mouse, keyboard). Organizations should anticipate learners with skill deficiencies in this area. A basic introductory tutorial (preferably face-to-face) should be developed to build learner skills.

- *The Internet.* This second level of orientation involves connecting to the Internet, using a browser (Netscape, Internet Explorer), understanding navigation structure, following links and returning back to the starting point, viewing multimedia sites (video, software demos, audio), downloading files, and so forth. Many excellent (and free) tutorials are available on the Internet to build student knowledge and skill in this area. A simple search for "Internet tutorials" yields useful resources for organizations to offer learners.

- *The virtual classroom.* At this stage, students are actually involved in an online course. Here the student makes the critical transition from "bricks" to "clicks" orientation. Students experience a shift in perspective of what it means to learn. Anchor points, such as a physical classroom, are replaced by the course home page, email with the instructor, and file sharing with other students. The course instructor is responsible for ensuring students are properly oriented to the virtual classroom. It may be helpful for learners new to the online environment to have access to the course management system a week before the course begins. This will allow the learner time to become acquainted with the virtual classroom and (as mentioned in the next point) the course software.

- *The course software.* This area of orientation may occur at the same time as the student is orientating to the virtual classroom. Here the student experiences the tools of online learning. The various applications needed to learn online are chat, discussion, voice-over IP, whiteboard, file sharing, email, and peer-to-peer software.

- *The instructor and students.* This level is very similar to a regular classroom course. Students experience a period of orientation to an instructor's style and to the personalities of other students. In some cases, depending on the level of interaction in the course, students may not fully orient to other students (or even the instructor). Instructors may find it useful to schedule limited activities over the first several days. Often, technical problems or misunderstandings result in students accessing courses late.

- *The course material.* This level is also similar to a regular classroom course. Ideally, a student should spend most of his or her time at this level. This is where the interaction with course content occurs, and this is the most critical part of the learning process. An instructor should attempt to move students into this area of orientation as quickly as possible.

Students beginning their first online course will be at various stages of orientation. It is critical that an instructor be able to accommodate students at different levels of comfort with e-learning. Students who have little or no knowledge of computers will enter a course at level one or two. Students who are familiar with online learning will enter a new course at level five or six. Learning and interaction with course content begin almost immediately. An instructor who is sensitive to various orientations can assist students by personalizing instruction. For example, a student at level one may be offered a remedial resource/course on how computers and the Internet work. A student at level six may be given additional course materials (beyond the focus of the course) with which to interact.

A critical aspect of any course is the initial orientation. This orientation may occur entirely online or, if suitable, in a face-to-face class. The session should include the following:

- An assessment of students' familiarity with computers/technology/ online learning;
- Introductions of instructor and students;
- All software/plug-ins needed for the course;
- Review of where important course documents are kept (course outline, class schedules, assignment due dates, test dates);
- Instructor's "rules." All instructors have rules that they want students to follow. These should be discussed in the first class;

- Netiquette guidelines for the course; and
- Student resources (information on technical support, learning support, and so on).

A significant part of the orientation process for new online students is learning how to use various communication tools. Chat, discussion, whiteboards, listservs, assignment posting repository, and emails are all unique features of online learning that help to create a connection between students and between students and course materials. Students should be encouraged to use various communication tools early into the course. It is advisable for the instructor to plan specific activities using different tools. Working through activities using communication tools helps students to become familiar with the potential of each tool.

Developing a Study Plan

After learners have acclimated to the online course, instructors should encourage new online learners to develop a study plan. A study plan helps to guide the learner through the process of learning online (similar to setting goals). A learner's study plan should answer the following questions:

- When will I study?
- Where will I study (at home/at the office)?
- How many hours a week can I commit?
- What are competing priorities in my life? How can I work around these?
- How will I contact the instructor/fellow students (phone, email, chat, discussion forum)?
- When will I evaluate my study plan to see if it is working?

Once learners have progressed through all of the stages of orientation, they begin to interact with the course material. Discussion questions, chat, voice-over IP, file sharing—all draw the student in. After learners have participated in an online environment for a while, they come to the realizations that most e-learners do: "I have a voice online!" "I have better access to the instructor, better access to classmates, and a more secure environment to express my ideas!" At this stage, technology is no longer the barrier to effective learning, but the enhancer.

Communication is the heart of learning. As students acclimate to the dynamics of online communication tools, they no longer rely solely on instructors to "give" knowledge. Students begin to realize that learning happens while interacting with peers and with course material. The instructor can then perform the role of moderating and guiding.

ESSENTIAL SKILLS AND KNOWLEDGE FOR E-INSTRUCTORS

The instructor is perhaps the greatest determinant of student success. Students new to the online environment rely heavily on the instructor to be an anchor. A common concern with students first starting to learn on the Internet is the unmooring. Traditional classrooms have many points of anchoring the student—physical points like students, desks, chalkboard, and walls. Yet online learning does not have the physical component. Online is open; one minute a student is surfing a European entertainment site, and the next minute he or she is reading the local weather forecast. This very experience is a benefit of the Internet, but to new students it is intimidating and overwhelming.

Skills and knowledge needed for instructors online are similar to those needed in a classroom. What is different, however, is *how* these are practiced online. For example, critical skills, such as establishing rapport, fostering communication, creating a student-friendly environment, permitting flexibility, and encouraging experimentation (and accepting failure as part of the learning process), are important regardless of delivery method. When these skills are practiced online, however, instructors need to rely on technology tools.

Rapport: Connecting with Students

For this reason the first goal of an instructor is to connect with the student (establish rapport); if no connection is made, the student may feel isolated. Establishing rapport may be as simple as sending students a personalized email wishing them success or the instructor sharing personal stories. By establishing a connection with students, an instructor can ensure students that he or she is "there" and that everything is working (course software, connection to instructor).

It is also very important that instructors realize the humanity of online learners. An instructor online does not have traditional face-to-face contact. It is important, therefore, that an instructor does not see students as merely a user name that appears in chat rooms and discussion boards.

Humanizing a course involves the instructor sharing personal life experiences, incorporating appropriate humor, and encouraging students to do the same. Some instructors use personal web pages as a place where learners can post pictures and share stories. These types of resources may make some people uncomfortable (they may prefer the anonymity the Internet offers), and so instructors should not make personal sharing a requirement of the course.

Communicating Online

Instructors must be skilled at communication. Communication should be constant. New online instructors quickly notice how small errors of communication can paralyze a class. In a traditional classroom, an assignment that is not communicated clearly can be clarified as the instructor "adds on" through in-class discussions. Online communication is often only one-way. Concepts need to be communicated clearly the first time. This may involve extra preparation time for the instructor. In fact, many instructors comment on how much more preparation and organization are involved in online classes compared to regular classrooms.

The structure of the course will impact on the forms of communication used. An academic setting will probably focus on time—everyone starts/finishes at the same time. Synchronous discussion and delivery tools may be used more prominently in this format. A business may focus on employees gaining knowledge in a certain area, and the structure of the course may allow for continuous intake (students can enter at any time) or flexible exit (students can complete the course ahead/behind schedule). This way employees can gain knowledge when needed. This type of course structure is more conducive to asynchronous learning. Discussion forums, listservs, text, video-on-demand, and others are ideally suited for the needs of "knowledge learners."

Theoretically, students should be successful learners on the Internet because of the *potential* for individualization. Students are not as readily lost in the digital shuffle as they are in a classroom. Digitally, every student has an equal voice. Many students who have been involved in an online course list ready access to the instructor as one of the main benefits. Instructors should realize that individualization is a characteristic of the Internet that needs to be incorporated into online learning.

Allowing students to create their own web space, personal emails, and individual voices in chat and discussion forums all create an individualized medium. Developments in instructional design and pre-tests also promise to create content individualization. An additional benefit is the ability for mastery learning; students can review/watch/read until the concept has been learned.

Instructor as Creator of Online Environment

Instructors should see themselves as the creator and curator of the online learning environment. The feel of the digital classroom, the depth of student interactions, the frequency of contact with course material, and the liveliness of the discussions are all influenced by the instructor.

It is the responsibility of the instructor to create and maintain an environment where each student feels secure and respected. Many students may be uncomfortable learning with technology, and a negative class environment (impersonal or the instructor is never present or accessible) may drive them away from online learning.

The Importance of Flexibility

Instructors should also be flexible. Most students who learn online do so because their schedule does not allow attending a brick and mortar school. Students appreciate the flexibility of learning online, and an instructor should make every attempt to build in flexibility. Students involved in a class may also be from different areas of the world and in different time zones. This is also a situation that an instructor should be aware of, especially when planning synchronous activities. Cultural differences should be considered as well. Assertive behaviors or contradicting an instructor may be seen as taboo in other cultures. Certain cultures may also favor either individual or group work.

Instructors can add flexibility into courses by evaluating each student's situation individually. Assignment deadlines and submission formats, attendance requirements at synchronous events, and other requirements should all be flexible if students have unique requests. An instructor should, however, be careful in providing too much flexibility. If the students perceive that assignments, tests, and course work can be changed readily, they may seek extensions that allow them to procrastinate about completing assignments. Flexibility should allow learners the ability to have their unique situations reflected in course work, but not to the point of hampering the learner or overwhelming the instructor.

In a digital classroom, the instructor is best described as being a guide who directs student exposure to various resources. Learning online allows students to explore, familiarizing themselves with course resources, following links, and getting involved in group discussions. Exploration is one of the strengths of online learning. A student can explore what she or he wants. Online students control their interaction with course material (compared to a classroom environment, where an instructor often controls interaction with material). Often an instructor only becomes involved when the direction students are going needs to be changed or an opportunity exists to summarize discussion points and link them to course learning objectives.

The Value of Experimentation and Failure

Finally, an instructor should be prepared to experiment. Failure (of both instructor and student) is an integral part of any learning experience. In fact, much learning can result from a failure. Instructors should be willing to try new resources, new techniques, and new styles of delivery. Experimentation is *critical* in online learning. Instructors who experiment intelligently (that is, their experimentation does not harm the student's learning experience) will slowly move toward the creation of an online persona and classroom that works for them and for their students. Once students see that failure (incorrect answers, solutions to problems that don't "work") is an accepted part of learning online, they may become more comfortable in this environment. As the student's comfort level increases, he or she may also become more adventurous, trying new things and becoming more actively involved. This transformation (from tentative contributor to confident explorer) is a rewarding outcome for instructors.

Effective planning, organizing, and delivery of online courses can significantly impact student success. Yet it is important for instructors to realize that some students will dislike learning online. They may not like the technology, they may feel they are not able to learn online, or the environment may be too foreign. Instructors need to be prepared for this.

Table 8.2 highlights some ways that learners can prepare for online courses and ways that instructors can assist them.

Table 8.2. Learner and Instructor Preparation

Learner	Instructor
Identify perceptions of what it means to learn online.	Take an online course. See what it is like from a student perspective. Understanding the student experience is critical for instructors.
Be patient. Realize that before learning can happen online, a learner must first learn the online environment.	Create a "personable" online image. Take time to engage students in appropriate conversation that is not just course related.
Create a study plan.	Create a space for students to express themselves; post pictures, talk about their likes/dislikes/hobbies, and so forth. This is the online version of the student lounge.
Explore. Familiarize yourself with course resources, follow links, get involved in discussions.	Establish rapport early. Contact students through email, phone, and other means. Let them know you exist.
Study. Set aside regular time to work on course information. Instructors should give estimated guidelines of study expectations each week.	Treat students differently. Take more time with students who are struggling.
Communicate. Communicate with the instructor and with other students. Let the instructor know of any problems quickly.	Don't assume anything. Spell it out in the course outline, for example, how often do you answer emails? In what format should assignments be submitted? Who do they contact if the network is down? When can help be contacted? How should contact be made?
Apply what has been learned. Application is the equivalent of learning it again.	Create "rich course resources." Use the strength of the Internet. List resources, links, communities, extra reading, and so forth.
Be willing to share personal/ educational experiences as part of the process of learning.	Build a list of support resources that learners of varying online experiences can explore. These may include links to "netiquette" articles, chat phrases, or technology tutorials. This serves as a "remedial resource."

Table 8.2. Learner and Instructor Preparation, Cont'd

Learner	Instructor
Know why you are taking the course, and focus on the rewards of successfully completing coursework.	Attach marks to critical learning points.
Practice critical thinking and decision making as part of learning. Realize that mistakes are often the best teachers.	Allow students time to reflect on the new online environment and on course content.

An understanding of the student's process of orientation, excellent teaching/communication/facilitation skills, and clearly defined expectations help to ensure student success. It is necessary to realize that excellent online learning is an extension of many of the principles of excellent classroom/distance/self-directed learning. In order for online learners to succeed, they must practice the foundational skills that are needed for learning in any situation. These include time on task, application, and motivation. These aspects of learning do not change, regardless of the environment in which learning occurs.

Most students have the ability to do well in an online learning environment. Many, however, do not succeed because of barriers or restrictions that impede student interaction with course content. It is important that the organization and the instructor be focused on creating a level of student preparation that ensures student success. The potentials of online learning—lower costs, highly trained staff, and increased profits—are only realized when learners and instructors are properly prepared to engage in the dynamics of technology-enabled learning.

About the Authors

George Siemens and Stephen Yurkiw are founders of eLogios Inc., a corporation that specializes in e-learning content and multimedia development. They can be reached at gsiemens@elogios.com or syurkiw@elogios.com. For e-learning information and resources, visit: www.elearnspace.org.

Chapter 9

The e-Learning Instructor*

Creator of Collegial Environments and Facilitator of Autonomous Learning

Paul B. Carr and Michael K. Ponton

Comments from e-Learners

"The best part was talking to other employees in the chat sessions."

"More chat time!"

"The online instructor needs to be accessible off-line."

RECENT RESEARCH HAS SUGGESTED that creating a sense of community within the e-learning platform will enhance the learning experience. Although sense of community among learners is an important construct, e-learning proponents may not fully consider the opportunity that exists to develop learner autonomy and the importance of creating collegial environments when doing so.

The premise of this chapter is that the e-learning environment is not a crippled avenue for the facilitation of learning (as compared to face-to-face environments) when the facilitator considers the im-

---

*Many of the ideas presented in this chapter were first presented at the 16th International Symposium on Self-Directed Learning held in Boynton Beach, Florida, February 7–9, 2002. The authors would like to thank Ms. Connie Ingram of Regent University for her contributions to this effort.

portance of enhancing learner autonomy. In essence, the e-learning environment can be viewed as a superior method for the facilitation of learner autonomy when one considers the potential for learner/facilitator interaction, or lack thereof, during the white space in asynchronous learning.

This chapter will present particular considerations when creating collegial environments in the e-learning platform that may enhance a learner's engagement in the conative factors of desire, initiative, resourcefulness, and persistence in learning, thereby developing learner autonomy. Creating environments conducive to autonomous learning is the quintessential goal of the facilitator of learning and is especially appropriate in e-learning. The basic tenets of creating collegial environments in the e-learning platform will be discussed, along with a pragmatic approach to leading the learner from dysfunctional learner dependence to functional learner autonomy in the asynchronous e-learning environment.

INTRODUCTION

Working for a large and growing company in an industry that requires continual training for its employees, John (who is in charge of all training) is quite frustrated. Despite his best efforts to structure e-learning opportunities for employees, he has found that great coaxing (or even mandating) is required to foster participation. Unless e-learning courses are available, and perhaps required, employees do not facilitate their own learning when needs arise. Consequently, his training budget is skyrocketing and he does not know what to do.

John works from a model that he feels is the most advanced possible. e-Learning courses are highly structured so that the student is carefully guided through each aspect of the course, whereby the instructor serves as the authority figure and is "in charge" of all learning. The training that employees receive is very effective in that the content knowledge of the course is adequately received by the employees; however, the graduates of such courses do not willingly seek out new learning as new job demands evolve. Consequently,

John spends a great deal of time and money identifying new job demands, finding instructors who are authorities, creating highly structured e-learning courses, finding ways to mandate employee participation, paying instructors to carefully control all facets of learning, and managing all aspects of training old and new employees.

If only the employees were autonomous enough to exhibit desire, initiative, resourcefulness, and persistence in job-related learning! Perhaps an e-learning course can do more than just transmit information—perhaps an e-learning course can change the characteristics of the learner. But what can an instructor do to create autonomous learners? What type of relationship should exist between an instructor and a student to achieve this goal?

OVERVIEW OF LEARNER AUTONOMY

One of the most important issues in adult education today is learning and how people learn. Chene (1983) asserts the following:

"Adult education in industrialized countries has been largely inspired by progressive and humanistic philosophy and has been developed on the assumptions of individual freedom, responsibility, and dignity. One of the central concepts found in the ideology of adult education as well as in practice is that of autonomy." (p. 38)

Confessore (1992) states that desire, initiative, resourcefulness, and persistence are conative factors that constitute the construct of autonomous learning. Ponton, Carr, and Confessore (1999) assert that learner autonomy is reflected in the cognitive and affective characteristics of the learner and is a precursor to conative learning, that is, intentional autonomous learning.

The importance of learner autonomy is not limited to the field of education however. Bandura (1997) states, "Changing realities are placing a premium on the capability for self-directed learning throughout the life span. . . . Self-development with age partly determines whether the expanded life span is lived self-fulfillingly or apathetically. These changing realities call for lifelong learners" (p. 227). Bandura further asserts, "[The] development of capabilities for self-directedness enables individuals not only to continue their intellectual growth beyond their formal education but to advance the nature and quality of their life pursuits" (p. 227).

Often these life pursuits involve taking a college course or perhaps pursuing a post-secondary degree. When pursuing higher education, the learner of today is provided with an assortment of academic opportunities and educational delivery systems. In essence, the learner now has the following choices: (1) local or same place at the same time learning; (2) synchronous or different places at the same time; and (3) asynchronous or different places at different times (Crumpacker, 2001). However, the word "distance" in distance learning is not restricted to the connotation of the geographical separation between student and educator; the construct of "distance" may be interpreted in light of the following assertion (Distance-Educator.com, www.distance-educator.com/index1a101600.phtml):

"Educators structuring the process of teaching and students taking responsibility for their learning define distance in education. The more teaching is structured, the more there is distance between a teacher and an educator. The more students take initiative for their learning, and control and influence their own education[,] the less distance is introduced." (para. 1)

CREATING ENVIRONMENTS CONDUCIVE TO LEARNING

Davis (1993) outlines several teaching strategies that are available to the instructor: (1) training and coaching; (2) lecturing and explaining; (3) inquiry and discovery; (4) groups and teams; and (5) experience and reflection. There are facets of some strategies interspersed with others, and the opportunity for e-learning adds complexity to the choices. Davis suggests that the degree to which an instructional strategy is deemed appropriate is a function of how fully the characteristics of the student, setting, and subject are considered. The consideration of student involves an assessment of the student's academic skills, emotional development, cognitive skills (for example, the ability to motivate and regulate personal behavior), perceptual modality, information processing style, intelligence, values, and goals. The setting includes not only the physical and social space of the classroom but also the culture and mission of the institution. The subject refers to both the explicit subject as reflected in the course description and role within the curriculum as well as implicit subjects, that is, other salient educational objectives such as the fostering of learner autonomy. Fostering learner autonomy is presently proposed as being of paramount importance, as it places learners in a position to effect change in their lives after formal education is completed, as well as during the learning endeavor itself.

The e-Learning Platform Is
Not a Crippled Mode of Learning

In general, most instructional strategies can be dysfunctional (that is, crippled) if the nature of the student, setting, and subject matter is not fully considered. Only through a clear understanding of the extent of the expected learning can an instructor develop a logical instructional strategy. With this being stated, e-learning environments can be just as dysfunctional as any face-to-face learning activity, provided the intent of the strategy is not completely understood.

There has been a great deal of research conducted regarding models of online delivery since the inception of the e-learning platform. The research of Holmberg (1989), Keegan (1990), Moore and Kearsley (1996), Peters (1998), and Sonwalker (2001) has concentrated largely on defining the field of e-learning and developing models for delivery. It appears as though a great deal of research has been conducted from the posture of effective teaching and course delivery, that is, the pedagogical posture. One facet of the e-learning environment that appears to have been neglected is the manner in which environments conducive to learner autonomy are created. In essence, the focus appears to be on the correct methods to construct and deliver courses utilizing the e-learning platform. Creating collegial environments in the e-learning platform is more concerned with the development of desirable learner characteristics and not solely on content transmission.

Colleagues and Autonomy

One's colleagues are those persons with whom an individual chooses to collaborate based on the knowledge, skills, and strategies that they are able to contribute to the "collegial" enterprise of accomplishing shared goals. An important characteristic of colleagues is their learner autonomy. In a team environment, the development of new ideas that expand knowledge and understanding requires a great deal of learning via thinking. Colleagues who are able to contribute to team activities in a meaningful manner are those who are able to muster the requisite cognitive inducements that facilitate an independence of thought. Such inducements are evidenced by the desire, initiative, resourcefulness, and persistence that are manifest in their autonomous learning.

Donna Meyer developed a three-factor construct of desire in learner autonomy (that is, precursors to intentional learning) that include a perception of basic freedoms, power management, and change skills. Within this construct, a learner is able to manifest a desire to learn (or, in fact, engage in any intentional activity) when these factors are present. Initiative in autonomous learning, formalized by Michael Ponton, refers to a syndrome of behaviors that include goal-directedness, action-orientation, persistence in overcoming obstacles, an active approach to problem solving, and self-startedness (Ponton & Carr, 2002). Paul Carr contextualized Michael Rosenbaum's construct of "learned resourcefulness" to autonomous learning and developed a four-factor construct of resourcefulness that includes the following behaviors: (1) prioritizing learning over non-learning activities; (2) choosing to engage in learning activities when non-learning activities are available;

(3) anticipating the future benefits of current learning; and (4) solving problems associated with learning activities. Gail Derrick has defined persistence in autonomous learning as involving volition, self-regulation, and goal-directedness.

CREATING COLLEGIAL ENVIRONMENTS

Ponton and Carr (2000) argue that the instructor can foster learner autonomy by developing instructional strategies that address the critical facets of these four conative factors. Such facets include helping the student to understand that (1) learning can lead to the accomplishment of desired outcomes throughout life, (2) accomplishing desired outcomes is predicated upon working toward carefully chosen goals, and (3) responsibility for one's own learning resides with the learner. These fundamental assertions provide a foundation for additional instructional strategies that address the unique features of the conative factors.

The development of a collegial environment is based on two distinct dimensions. The first refers to the mutual understanding between the instructor and the student that they are interdependent members of a team with common goals—one major goal being the development of learner autonomy. However, the goal of autonomy should not remain an implicit one. The fostering of autonomy should be an explicit goal of the course whereby the instructor informs the students that they must work diligently together as colleagues in pursuit of this goal. The role of the instructor is to develop an appropriate instructional strategy that fosters autonomy, and the student's role is to fully engage in the learning activity cognitively, affectively, and conatively. The second dimension of the collegial environment is based on the anticipated result of learners transforming into competent individuals with whom the instructor will someday collaborate. This anticipated future state affects the current instructional environment, as it places true learning and cognitive development at the pinnacle of the academic endeavor, thereby creating the second dimension of the collegial environment. However, such future states do not have to extend far into the future. Students can transform into worthy colleagues who create desired learning for both themselves *and* the instructor within the framework of the current course. Creating collegial environments conducive to the development of learner autonomy should be considered a goal for all learning strategies.

Creating collegial environments conducive to autonomous learning is the quintessential goal of the facilitator of learning in the asynchronous e-learning platform. The instructor (more favorably referred to as the facilitator) concentrates on enhancing learner independence and autonomy and views the learning environment and assessment tasks as vehicles for the enhancement of learner autonomy. The premise of creating collegial environments is based largely on the view that the learners are colleagues in the learning endeavor and that the learners are assuming the responsibility for their learning achievements. The facilitator interacts with the learner according to the needs of the learner and the learner's level of autonomy. The premise is the creation of *individual* environments that may lead to an increasingly autonomous learner. The particular content learned within the constraints of the course act as vehicles for enhancing learner autonomy and developing self-regulated learners.

Grow (1991, 1996) devised the staged self-directed learning model wherein the instructor's purpose is to match interaction to the learner's stage of self-direction, thereby preparing the learner to advance to higher stages. He offers four stages to categorize a learner's level of self-direction: (1) dependent; (2) interested; (3) involved; and (4) self-directed. Grow posits that each stage suggests an appropriate instructional role that will lead to enhanced learning and movement from a state of learner dependency to independence. Confessore and Carr (2001) suggest that learner autonomy resides along a continuum, with dysfunctional learner dependence on one extreme and dysfunctional learner independence on the other—functional learner autonomy is in the center of this continuum. The dependence extreme is viewed as dysfunctional because the learner requires a prescribed environment ad infinitum, while the independence extreme is dysfunctional because the learner completely removes the opportunity for social learning (Rovai & Lucking, 2000).

Creating collegial environments in the e-learning platform requires the facilitator to ascertain the learner's level of autonomy, thereby providing the appropriate support for the learner. An important role of the facilitator is to continually indicate to the student that an important goal of the learning endeavor is to have the learner leave the formal educational course/program as an autonomous learner. During the learning endeavor, the learner and the facilitator become colleagues and advocates for continued success. In essence, the learner should become highly autonomous and not require the assistance of an instructor for additional learning endeavors unless he or she chooses to do so. Certainly, this scenario is a lofty goal, even for a collegial learning endeavor.

Creating collegial environments in the asynchronous e-learning platform begins with the learner knowing that the facilitator is his or her advocate for success in the endeavor. The facilitator should ask the learner to create goals and strategic outcomes for the e-learning endeavor which are in concert with the goals and strategic outcomes of the course/program. The facilitator should then ascertain the learner's comfort level regarding independent learning. By this, the facilitator should ascertain whether the learner requires prescriptive instruction or if he or she is comfortable in relative autonomy. One of the goals associated with creating collegial environments is that the learner knows that he or she is striving to become increasingly autonomous whereby the assessment tasks are avenues for mastery experiences that increase learner autonomy. In essence, the learner must be aware of the process prior to and during the endeavor.

In fostering autonomy, the facilitator should make judicious use of the detachment afforded in an e-learning environment. Through online discussions, instructors should consciously determine if and when to interject. In face-to-face learning activities, the real time white space can be an awkward situation for both the students and instructor; however, in an asynchronous delivery system, temporal delays may go undetected. This does not mean that the instructor should not establish regular contact with students, but a facilitator of autonomy should not allow students to develop a dependency on formalized instruction by supplying readymade answers. From this perspective, detachment can be viewed as an intentional instructional strategy and not pedagogical negligence.

A Model for Creating Collegial Environments in the e-Learning Platform

Creating collegial environments in the e-learning platform is very simply about the learner's needs—not the instructor's. Some suggestions for the e-learning facilitator (not in order of significance) to enable a fostering of a collegial environment follow.

Show Continual Respect for the Learner and the Endeavor Itself. Rogers (as cited in Tennant, 1997, p. 16) indicates that good facilitators of learning value the learner's feelings and opinions and consider the learner trustworthy. In this regard, facilitators should (1) attempt to have the learners visualize the reality of their desired learning outcomes, thereby adding value to the endeavor itself, and (2) display respect for their students' values as manifest in interactions and through the development of appropriate instructional strategies that foster autonomy, thereby facilitating lifelong change.

Ask for Buy-In. Facilitators should (1) help learners to become aware of the processes involved with self-regulated learning and introduce the learners to the behaviors associated with the conative factors of desire, resourcefulness, initiative, and persistence in learning, and (2) attempt to develop student self-efficacy by assisting students to attribute learning accomplishments to increases in personal ability.

Create a Safe Climate for Learning. Facilitators should help learners to understand that the instructor is their advocate for success in the learning endeavor. In essence, the facilitator can act as a change agent by creating an environment conducive to student growth.

Ascertain the Needs, Intentions, and Goals of the Learners. Facilitators should help students to become aware that the goals and strategic outcomes for the learning endeavor are aligned with their personal goals and desired outcomes. In essence, course requirements and strategies should pass each student's "So what?" test of importance. If the learner can relate course goals (such as fostering autonomy) to personal goals (such as becoming an agent of desired change), then a personal commitment is fostered by the student, and the assessment task becomes a vehicle for promoting self-direction.

Autonomy Begins with Relationships. The relationship between the learners and the facilitator is vastly important, especially in the e-learning environment. Facilitators should be certain that learners know they are available for support, direction, and concerns that arise.

Remember How You Felt when You Were a Student and Let the Learners Know You Remember. Learning can induce stress due to the processes of extending understanding, managing life demands, and mustering the cognitive strategies required for continual participation. Learners will receive great comfort throughout this growth process if they realize that facilitators recognize such stressors through reflection on their own past learning endeavors and use this information to help students to interpret such stressors as transient processes that will subside when learning abilities and cognitive strategies are refined.

Utilize All Available Technology. The e-learning platform can be a superior mode of learning when married with additional technology. Many e-learning models utilize only Internet-based tools; however, creative uses of other technologies can profoundly enhance the learning endeavor. As a simple example, it often helps the facilitator to opt for Ma Bell's instrument and make a telephone call to the learner.

Be a Coach—If You Quit, I Will Be Offended. Instructors should let learners know that they can and will succeed in their learning goals through diligent efforts. Facilitators should adopt the posture that excellence is expected from the learners and understand that collegiality requires both parties to desire and work toward academic excellence. Part of the collegial enterprise is fostering a sense of interdependent roles that will lead to learner independence.

If instructors approach students not from the perspective of customers or clients to whom knowledge is "given," but rather from the perspective that a goal is to develop competent and autonomous learners with whom the facilitator may collaborate as a colleague, then the instructional approach and learning environment become decidedly different. Interactions are no longer limited to a façade that teaching and learning are occurring, as this will not foster the true competency on which instructors may one day rely. Instructors must take the posture that the most relevant "subject" to be taught is the development of learner autonomy within students. Only when this lesson is learned well will students transform into the persons instructors will choose to have as colleagues.

With this consideration in mind, e-learning can serve as an effective medium through which learner autonomy is fostered. This does not mean that such autonomy cannot be fostered in face-to-face experiences; however, because of the "white space" (that is, the lack of prescriptive presentations at exceedingly high levels of detail) in a typical e-learning lesson, a considerable opportunity exists for students to fill the space as they deem relevant. The lack of prescription and the availability of numerous online resources provide the opportunity for autonomous learning to occur. Thus, the instructional strategy of the instructor should be to use the technology to foster the conative factors of desire, initiative, resourcefulness, and persistence (see Ponton & Carr, 2000) rather than attempt to create highly prescriptive environments that, in the end, allow the student very little volitional control.

Of course some subjects do require a great deal of detail in the e-learning lessons proffered (for example, statistics). There is no one instructional strategy that works in every situation. However, using the above as a critical lens through which instructors search for opportunities to enhance learner autonomy will provide a useful mechanism for identifying courses that can incorporate less prescription. In this manner, the e-learning environment can be used to effectively enhance learner autonomy, thereby creating an environment that serves to develop colleagues for future mutual achievement. The lack of prescription is truly a collegial environment, as both the instructor and student form a team with the common goal of enabling the student to become a master autonomous learner within the context of the curriculum.

CONCLUSION

Creating collegial environments conducive to autonomous learning is the quintessential goal of the facilitator of learning in the asynchronous e-learning platform. While many facilitators of learning are concerned with constructs such as building classroom community at a distance (Rovai & Lucking, 2000), the premise of creating collegial environments in the e-learning platform is concerned with creating avenues for the learner to develop as an autonomous learner. Additionally, it should be noted that the e-learning platform is not a crippled mode of learning when compared with local (that is, face-to-face) learning environments—both represent different strategies that can facilitate learning when the student, subject, and setting are adequately considered. However, in an e-learning endeavor it is presently argued that the instructor has a considerable opportunity to enhance learner autonomy if the "white space in learning" is used to academically stretch the learner by providing the time to think critically and reflectively (Confessore & Carr, 2001).

The construct of creating collegial environments in the e-learning platform is about relationships between the instructor and individual learners while the instructor serves as an advocate for student learning and success. A paramount consideration in creating collegial environments is to ascertain the initial level of autonomy of the learners and provide the appropriate level of facilitation and support required for each individual student.

References

Bandura, A. (1997). *Self-efficacy: The exercise of control.* New York: W.H. Freeman and Company.

Chene, A. (1983). The concept of autonomy in adult education: A philosophical discussion. *Adult Education Quarterly, 34*(1), 38–47.

Confessore, G.J. (1992). An introduction to the study of self-directed learning. In G.J. Confessore & S.J. Confessore (Eds.), *Guideposts to self-directed learning: Expert commentary on essential concepts* (pp. 1–6). King of Prussia, PA: Organization Design and Development.

Confessore, G.J., & Carr, P.B. (2001, February). *Autonomous learning and the white-space: The staged self-directed learning model.* Paper presented at VIII Seminario Cientifico Sobre la Calidad de la Educacion: Intercambio de Experiencis de Professionales Cubanos y Nortamericanos. Havana, Cuba.

Crumpacker, N. (2001). Faculty pedagogical approach, skill and motivation in today's distance education milieu. *Online Journal of Distance Learning Administration, IV*(IV). [Retrieved January 05, 2002, from www.westga.edu/~distance/ojdla/winter44/crumpacker44.html]

Davis, J.R. (1993). *Better teaching more learning: Strategies for success in post-secondary settings.* Phoenix, AZ: American Council on Education and The Oryx Press.

Grow, G. (1991/1996). Teaching learners to be self-directed. *Adult Education Quarterly, 41*(3), 125–149. [Expanded version available online at www.longleaf.net/ggrow]

Holmberg, B. (1989). *Theory and practice of distance education.* London: Routledge.

Keegan, D. (1990). Open learning: Concepts and costs, successes and failures. In R. Atkinson & C. McBeath (Eds.), *Open learning and new technology* (pp. 230–243). Perth, Australia: ASET/Murdoch University.

Moore, M., & Kearsley, G. (1996). *Distance education: A systems view.* Belmont, CA: Wadsworth.

Peters, O. (1998). *Learning and teaching in distance education: Analysis and interpretations from an international perspective.* London: Kogan Page.

Ponton, M.K., & Carr, P.B. (2000). Understanding and promoting autonomy in self-directed learning. *Current research in social psychology* [On-line], 5(19). [Available: www.uiowa.edu/~grpproc]

Ponton, M.K., & Carr, P.B. (2002). The development of instrumentation that measures an adult's intention to exhibit initiative and resourcefulness

Chapter 10

Preparing Your Learners for My e-Learning

An e-Learning Vendor's Point of View

Terrence R. Redding

Comments from e-Learners

"The orientation course never told us why we were doing this, this way."

"Working at my own pace helped me learn it better."

"It's too confusing at first."

"Don't give me a failing mark simply because I never finished the course. Maybe I learned what I needed without finishing."

EDUCATION AND TRAINING CONTENT delivered over the Internet are becoming more common. This chapter will focus on the core topic of preparing your learners for e-learning. It will include the following subtopics:

- Why do I have to worry about e-learning?
- Screening e-learners—or does one size fit all?
- Orienting e-learners—tell them what to expect.
- Removing barriers to e-learning—technical support.
- Where is the trainer in e-learning—subject-matter expert support?
- Validating training—from the e-learners' perspective.

This chapter will expose you to but one perspective on preparing your learners for e-learning. Previous and subsequent chapters will share other perspectives. However, one of the common threads for each of the authors included in this book is the commitment to the notion that all adult students are self-directed learners to one degree or other.

This chapter's particular perspective for preparing e-learners draws primarily on its author's five years of recent experience as the founding president and CEO of a for-profit distance education company. In particular it will focus on the practical aspects of working with adult e-learners to ensure they successfully complete professional continuing education courses delivered exclusively via the Internet.

WHY DO I HAVE TO WORRY ABOUT e-LEARNING?

The knowledge explosion is real. The need to learn new things and to stay current in a particular discipline is essential. The pace at which new knowledge is being created is literally mind-numbing. Consider Figure 10.1.

Figure 10.1. Learning Curve of the Information Age

The knowledge explosion - an increasingly steep learning curve.

100%	The Agricultural Age	The Industrial Age	The Informational Age
	10,000 Years	400 Years	50 Years
30%			
5%			
	5%	30%	100%

Of all that man knows, 5 percent was learned in the first 10,000 years, 25 percent was learned in 400 years, and 70 percent was learned in the last 50 years! To be successful, one must be a life-long learner, a high self-directed learner. Nations that value high self-directed learning will dominate the world.

Adapted with permission from the OnLine Training Institute, 2002.

The figure depicts the increase in man's knowledge across the Agricultural Age, 10,000 years in length, the Industrial Age, 400 years in length, and the beginning of the Information Age. It illustrates the rapid increase in the amount of knowledge possessed by mankind. Only 5 percent of the world's knowledge was acquired in the first 10,000 years. During this period the acquisition of knowledge can be described as occurring at a gradual, slow pace. During the four hundred years of the Industrial Age another 25 percent of the world's knowledge was acquired. Five times more knowledge was acquired in one twenty-fifth of the time. Thus, the pace of change during the Industrial Age can be described as occurring 125 times faster than it did during the Agricultural Age. However, in just the last fifty years, 70 percent of the world's knowledge was acquired, and the pace at which new knowledge is being produced is increasing—with no slowdown in sight.

The increase in knowledge requires that its distribution and assimilation be handled as efficiently as possible. The Internet was designed to serve several purposes, one of which was to be a method for storing in a distributed manner the knowledge of mankind. Converting a system designed for distributive storage to an information distribution system was not an obvious step. Originally, access to the Internet was limited to government, military, and educational research institutions. The cost of access was thought to be too prohibitive to permit universal access to ever occur. The commercialization of the Internet in the late 1980s and early 1990s changed that, permitting both commercial companies and private citizens full access and use of the Internet. Now only about thirty years old, the Internet has transformed the distribution of data and communications. Having an email address today is as important as having a postal address.

SCREENING E-LEARNERS— OR DOES ONE SIZE FIT ALL?

Various strategies are employed to match learners with content and style of learning with method of delivery. Elsewhere in this book these topics are discussed in some detail. This section addresses the obligation of the e-learning provider to screen all potential students and ensure that the content to be presented online is appropriately structured for most learners.

A key component of a successful e-learning operation is the screening of potential students. This is a people-intensive activity. Initial screening is best done over the phone by a training representative who understands the training products to be delivered, and whom those products have been designed to serve. The following subtopics will be discussed in this section:

- Course description;
- Course prerequisites;
- Costs;
- Completion policy; and
- Student support.

The reality is that most of the screening occurs through a series of email exchanges. The email exchange is normally initiated by a potential student after viewing a course description online. The screening process may occur over the phone. In both cases the format is virtually the same. Enough information must be exchanged to ensure the student is enrolling in the right course to satisfy his or her training needs.

The course description is important and should contain enough information to tell the student what is included in the training and who the training is structured for, list any prerequisites that must be met by students wishing to enroll, and list the course's cost. Often students are unfamiliar with the terminology associated with a particular subject to be taught and thus may not understand what is being offered and what prerequisites, if any, are required.

Content being taught in a given subject area is often organized as introductory, intermediate, or advanced. Some courses may attempt to expose a student to all three levels of material, while other curriculums may separate the content into three courses, with each course designed for students of varying background. For example, the introductory material may be suitable for all new hires in a particular profession. The intermediate material may be suitable for those who are assuming middle management roles. And, finally, the advanced material may be designed primarily for students in upper management who will engage in decision making and planning that will provide direction to the organization.

Identifying and articulating course prerequisites during the screening process is increasingly important when offering intermediate and advanced courses. The training manager is interested in placing students in the correct course level for at least three reasons. First, certain courses can only be taken by qualified people in the proper sequence. Second, students should often be grouped by years of experience, level of existing expertise, or skill level in order to engage some types of content. Third, some topics are so complex that members of the class must be of similar backgrounds in order to effectively interact with the content and one another.

The process of screening must include a method for evaluating costs. Most often costs are thought of in terms of a dollar value. But e-learning costs should also consider length of time, when time must be scheduled, level of effort, and other resources that must be committed to the learning process. Cost as a dollar amount is decreasing as a valued consideration. Time is increasingly the resource most limited in supply. Thus, when screening a potential student, the advisor must be able to describe how effective or efficient the e-learning experience is going to be.

A completion policy ensures that students exit the course at the appropriate point in time. If a completion policy has not been established, it is possible a student will remain in a course for an extended period of time trying to score 100 percent on the final comprehensive exam, when a score of 90 percent would have completely satisfied the course requirements.

Student support has to be tailored to meet the needs of the individual student. One size does not fit all. New students may require a substantial amount of help initially to access the course. Returning students may not even require a course orientation if courses offered have been standardized sufficiently. Student support will be covered elsewhere more thoroughly.

ORIENTING e-LEARNERS— TELL THEM WHAT TO EXPECT

e-Learning is still new. Most people have never taken an e-learning course over the Internet. And, even if they have, the variation in delivery methods, instructional designs, and technologies employed mean that each student may still not know what to expect.

At the beginning of an e-learning experience, it is important to tell the students what to expect. Provide a comprehensive outline of the knowledge they will encounter and the methods that will be used to explore and gain mastery over that knowledge. Provide the students with a clear understanding of what they are expected to do and what to expect as a response from the instructional system.

Setting the expectations of the student is one of the primary ways the instructor, or instructional design team, controls the learning environment. Six areas should be covered with every student as you set the expectations: time, place, content, method of instruction, technology, and support.

Time

Is the course self-paced (asynchronous) or does it meet on a schedule at a pre-set time (synchronous)? As indicated above, time considerations may be the key factor used by students to determine if and when they will enroll in an e-learning course. If enrollment is mandatory, it may also be the key factor for determining whether a student is satisfied or dissatisfied with the e-learning experience. Specifying the specific time to be engaged in a course may be acceptable if the content and instructional design selected for the subject are best handled in an asynchronous format.

Place

Where must the students be to participate in the course? Can they access the course from anywhere they have access to the Internet? Or are they required to be at work or at home when they access the course? Are they required to access the course from a specified computer lab or training facility? Each of these questions should be clearly answered for the student to ensure that their expectations are fully satisfied. Restricting access to a course by requiring the students to be in their individual cubicles, a training center, learning center, or specific computer lab may be frustrating for adult students who feel completely competent to engage in the course content from a location they have selected. However, specifying the place of instruction may be appropriate if the telephone is to be used during the course for conferencing or other resources specific to a particular place are needed to facilitate the instruction.

Content

Content is always an important element, and it must be fully explained to the student. Explaining what is to be learned, to what degree it will be learned, and who should learn it allows the students to confirm in their own minds that they are engaged in the correct course.

Method of Instruction

This is a key element of information for both the student and the instructional design team. Preparing e-learning courses is a time-consuming process. The level of deliberation and thought given to presenting information online should be intensive. The method of instruction should have "apparent logic," that is, it should appear logical to the students in order to foster confidence that they will effectively and efficiently learn what is being taught. Some methods of instruction are closed, permitting no interaction between the student and the instructor. These are typically self-paced courses, delivered via the Internet, limited in scope and complexity, but they can be highly effective. Other instructional designs can be intensely interactive, engaging the student and the instructor at increasing levels of complexity (Bensusan, 2002) on a wide variety of subjects asynchronously over an extended period of time.

Technology

Technology as a term is increasingly used to identify hardware, software, and networks. Its broader meaning includes all aspects (techniques) of an endeavor. It is used here under the narrower definition. e-Learners want to know whether their particular computers meet the technical specifications to be used in an online course. This is normally specified in terms of minimum requirements. e-Learners need to know whether their processor is fast enough, whether their operating system (OS) is supported, whether they have enough memory (random access memory or RAM), whether multimedia is required (sound, full, or limited motion video), and whether their connectivity (bandwidth to the Internet) is sufficiently high to accommodate the instructional strategy and technology. A good rule of thumb when designing an e-learning course is to intentionally use the least amount of technology required to deliver the optimum amount of appropriate content to the largest possible number of potential students.

Support

Support is too often not considered when preparing students for e-learning. Online courses have the reputation of being sterile and delivered in isolation, with no interaction between the student and another living soul. While most courses may be designed to be self-paced, with no student/instructor inaction, support is important, especially at the beginning of a course when students are first trying to gain access. The e-learning provider should always provide a help desk and student support, through the use of both email and telephone support. Initially, many students need to call a live person on the phone for help. But eventually they discover that email allows them to ask the questions when most convenient for the student, and that it also permits a deliberate written response that the student can then file and refer back to as needed. Often an e-learning provider may respond to an email message with a phone call—if that appears to be what is needed to meet the students' expectations and aid them in making progress in the course. New students always require more support than returning students. Often, knowing there is someone available to help is all that is needed. It permits the student to engage in the course and begin making progress through the content.

REMOVING BARRIERS TO e-LEARNING— TECHNICAL SUPPORT

e-Learning is a new experience for most students. For those new to e-learning, just the anxiety associated with turning on their computer, connecting to the Internet, and getting online may be enough of a barrier to make them avoid engaging in e-learning. Establishing a help desk and providing both email-based and telephone-based support can remove major barriers to e-learning.

Technical support and student screening can be performed by the same element of your organization or treated as completely separate functions. The OnLine Training Institute has found it helpful to combine the two functions. This approach increases the consistency of interaction between the online training group and the student. However you choose to structure your organization to prepare students for e-learning, you should understand that the preparation does not end with their enrollment. Continuing support is required for some students. The following items are the seven most common kinds of support questions asked for by students engaged in e-learning:

- How do I find the starting point for the course?
- How do I enter the user name and password to access the course?

- How can I get back to where I was in the course?
- How do I save my work?
- How can I resume work?
- How do I submit work?
- How do you know where I am in the course?

As an online course provider, I see all of these questions as barriers to learning. If the students are concerned with these questions, they are most likely not engaged in the educational content. Thus it is important to remove these learning barriers.

Most online training sites use what is known as a frequently asked questions (FAQ) list. Creating such a list and indexing it so that it is easy to use can reduce the number of questions normally fielded by your student help desk. Of course, it won't be able to answer all of them, and the number of questions you include in the FAQ list will increase over time. However, be cautioned, if you put too many question in the FAQ list you will eventually reach a point of diminishing return.

An effective way to use the FAQ list is to provide the student with the universal resource locator (URL) or address to the specific answer to the question in an email or telephone response. Over the phone, the student should be guided to the answer. In email, the student should be able to "click" on the link (select) and automatically have the browser go to the FAQ list on the web. This serves two purposes: First, it provides the answers to the students' questions, and second, it shows the students where to go to find answers to other questions as they arise.

WHERE IS THE TRAINER IN E-LEARNING—
SUBJECT-MATTER EXPERT SUPPORT

e-Learning, when done synchronously, always involves teachers with students. But the move is away from synchronous e-learning courses toward asynchronous courses that permit the student to control when and from where they engage in learning. The asynchronous format does not necessarily have to isolate the learner from the subject-matter expert. Three instructional design models for e-learning asynchronously have emerged. The first is one-on-one. The second is group one-on-one. The third is isolated learning with access to the instructor. Each of these three instructional models will be discussed in terms of how you prepare the student to engage in e-learning.

Students new to e-learning may believe they need an instructor to teach them the material. It is the instructional model they are most likely familiar with. It is the one most often used in public and parochial schools. Individuals with a home schooling background may, however, be very familiar with some aspects of e-learning and have little need for the instructor if the content is presented in a logical way.

The first model, one-on-one, may be used with self-paced online content that is presented in a modular fashion. The student is introduced to the e-learning instructor, who explains the various aspects of the course and describes how the student and instructor will interact. The course is designed as a self-paced course, with quizzes and tests automatically graded, with the grades reported to both the student and the instructor. The instructor monitors the student's progress through the course and consistently encourages the student to do his or her best. Some aspects of the course may require course work to be submitted to the instructor for subjective grading. This model is suitable for basic course work with students who may require more assistance. At OnLine Training (OLT) it is used in our basic adult education series to teach reading, writing, math, science, art, literature, and social studies. Under this model one instructor can monitor the progress of up to two hundred students a month who are moving through the same type of course. Interaction is consistent and occurs on a daily basis between actively engaged students and the instructor.

The second model is used with intermediate and advanced students who, once started in a course, require little or no contact with the instructor. In this model the course content is presented in a modular self-paced fashion with most of the course interaction and feedback provided only to the student. The instructor can monitor end-of-chapter and end-of-course exams and is readily available through email and a scheduled online chat room should a student have a question that requires a response from the subject-matter expert. This model allows one instructor, working full-time, to monitor up to one thousand students a month as they progress through the various courses.

The third model is used only for cram courses and test preparation courses. In these courses the student wishes to interact only with the online content by practicing exams and going through test practice material. The subject-matter expert is available but seldom receives email from or has contact with a student.

Because e-learning is done over a network, contact between the subject-matter experts and the students provides an opportunity to quickly receive feedback from students and improve course content based on student comments. Over time the course improves to the point where further improvements are less frequent.

VALIDATING TRAINING— FROM THE E-LEARNERS' PERSPECTIVE

Adult students typically decide what they wish to learn and to what degree they wish to learn. They decide when and where they will learn. In other words, adult students allocate their own learning resources. One important aspect of assuming responsibility for one's own learning is valuing the knowledge or deciding when you have learned enough.

In a traditional learning model, the instructor or the institutions set the standards. In an e-learning environment, often the students will want to decide not only what to learn, when to learn, and where to learn, but also to what degree they need to learn. It is up to the e-learning institution to satisfy this information need. Well-designed courses should include a method for assessing the level of learning that occurs. One way to do this is to provide a pre-test and a post-test. OnLine Training does this for our basic adult education students under the one-on-one model described above. This permits the student and the instructor to evaluate the state of a student's knowledge within a particular domain of knowledge at the beginning of a course of instruction. With this information, the instructor can advise the student as to how to approach the course and what to expect in terms of setting expectations for completing the course. By using a post-test, the instructor and the student can likewise determine whether, at the end of the course, the student has learned enough material to be able to pass a particular external exam such as the GED examination.

In other courses, such as OnLine Training's insurance licensing course, a method is provided for generating practice exams that closely resemble the kind of exam the state licensing agency will require the student to pass before issuing a state insurance license. Of course, it is essential that there be a high correlation on the exams administered by OLT at the end of a course and the "official" exam administered by an outside agency. Indeed, if an error is to be made, it is better to make the end-of-course exam administered online harder than the actual exam to reduce the possibility of failure on the actual exam.

In any case, whether the e-learning course provides a method for validating the educational content delivered during the course or not, the student will evaluate the course. It is a good policy to provide a formal mechanism for acquiring such student feedback. Normally two evaluations should be requested. The first should evaluate institutional support, and the second should evaluate the e-learning delivery.

SUMMARY

I have sought to provide an e-learning vendor's perspective on preparing students for e-learning, including a section that explored why you should be interested in e-learning. Of importance is the notion that knowledge is increasing faster and faster. There is more to know today than there was last year or ten years ago. In order to stay current in a chosen field, we all must engage in effective and efficient learning activities.

Screening learners was also addressed, as was the importance of orienting the learners on the content and the manner of instruction so that their expectations would be met. Of particular interest are ways an e-learning institution can control the learning environment, remove learning barriers, and provide students with appropriate levels and types of technical and instructional support.

Finally, validating instruction was addressed. In particular I stressed the importance of providing the e-learning students with the tools and information they would require in order to properly value the e-learning in which they have engaged.

References

Bensusan, G. (2002, January). Trochaic/iambic heptameter, *USDLA Journal,* 16(1).

OnLine Training. (2002, March). *Don't forget to fly the plane!* Keynote address by John Hibbs and panel presentation, WebCT conference, Melbourne, Australia

About the Author

Terrence R. Redding, Ph.D., president and CEO of OnLine Training, has been designing and teaching adult education courses since 1968. Redding is a past W. K. Kellogg Fellow and has a doctoral degree in adult and higher education. He has a master's in the psychology of education and is an honors graduate with a bachelor of science degree in education. His research has dealt with adult motivation theory and the origins of self-directed learning readiness. He has specialized in cognitive learning models and is the co-developer of the Honeycutt Redding Cognitive Task Analysis Model. More recently Redding has been the director of corporate training and corporate computer training at Palm Beach Atlantic College. He is the author of numerous refereed chapters dealing with adult learning theory. He is the founder of OnLine Training Institute.

Chapter 11

From the Learner's Perspective*

The e-Learners

QUOTES FROM E-LEARNERS

On Course Completion

"Don't give me a failing mark simply because I never finished the course. Maybe I learned what I needed without finishing."

"Let me explore things my own way. As long as I master the objectives, what does it matter if I read what is there or find the answers somewhere else."

"I don't want to be forced to contribute to threaded discussions to 'learn' from my peers. I don't think they know any more than I do."

---

*Editors' note: As part of our work on this book, the authors talked to a number of e-learners (both successful and not) concerning e-learning in general—what they found positive and negative about their experiences and what would help them to be more successful e-learners. Many of their thoughts are addressed in the various chapters, and you've seen a few of them heading each chapter. However, I thought you might like to hear them all in the e-learners' own words.

I found it difficult to systematize their thoughts, but gave it a try anyway. Some of the categories I've created relate directly to what we've covered in this book, while others are a bit more indirect. But whether you are a designer, manager, or implementer of e-learning, you should find many if not all of them to be most interesting. These are diamonds in the rough, presented for you to prospect and then polish into concepts that can help your e-learners succeed.

Good hunting!

"I took the course when I had the time."

"I like having a live instructor on the computer because then you have to be there."

"I hated writing on the bulletin board, but liked to read what others said. I think I learned a lot that way."

"Working at my own pace helped me learn it better."

On Course Organization

"Un-organized courses frustrate me. Give me signs about how the course is supposed to go."

"Don't organize the course according to your plan. Let me organize it the way I need to."

"I need to know what I'm going to learn before I can learn it."

"The flexibility was great."

On Course Design

"Give me a chance to read and a choice in what I read."

"Give me multiple ways to learn (threaded discussions, CD-ROMS, chat rooms, books, phone calls), then allow me to pick the way that works best for me."

"Don't overwhelm me with too much content. Give me activities to learn a little at a time."

"The course was no different than reading a textbook, except it wasn't as portable."

"I liked the games. They taught me more than anything else."

"I liked having the self-quizzes."

"Why would you have e-learning without video?"

"I liked how many graphics were used. Classrooms never use graphics like that."

"Why can't I print off the tables and charts?"

"The summaries at the end of each section were the best part. They were all I really needed to read."

"I liked how everything was divided into sections. It made it easier to understand."

"More links to outside information please."

"The quizzes."

"The study guide gave me something I could read in bed."

"The best part was talking to other employees in the chat sessions."

"The instructor should not be allowed to monitor the chat sessions."

"I always get sidetracked."

"The material didn't mean anything to me."

"More chat time!"

"The bulletin board activities really drove the point home. It's neat seeing how they do it in other parts of the company."

"We need more practice games."

"Don't make all the tests and games the same."

"Give me the option of using a textbook."

"More, and more complete outlines."

"It was interesting to collaborate with people from all over the company."

"I need hands-on learning if I'm going to learn it."

"I wanted something to take away from the e-learning, like the stuff you take away from a classroom."

"The time we spent doing the email collaboration was not well spent."

"I wanted to be able to do it from home."

"I liked being able to apply my own experiences in the threaded discussions."

Compared to a Classroom

"It was more interactive than a classroom."

"No war stories."

"I can't learn what nobody teaches me."

"I've always learned for myself and it's great that now that's OK."

"I need to be taught."

"I like an instructor to tell me what's important."

"I liked it, but I need classroom time too."

"I need face-to-face time."

"I liked not being pressured by an instructor."

"I need established class time."

"It's harder to focus when there is no class."

"I don't see why this is better than a classroom."

On User Interface

"I want total navigational freedom to and from anyplace at any time."

"It was good to be able to watch the demonstration over and over until I got it."

"It takes too much time to get online and get started, especially when you just wanted to look something up."

"I liked the ability to stop and start when I needed to."

On Preparation

"I get confused in the technical terminology from the start. Can't they use words to describe what the stuff is that isn't 'computerese'?"

"No one ever told me how to use the buttons."

"When I first started I needed someone to show me how—and then leave me alone."

"I got lost at the start and never got found again."

"It takes too long to learn what the software can and can't do."

"We need an in-class lecture at the beginning to show us how it works."

"It was too difficult learning how to log on the first time."

"The instructor should have explained how the software worked."

"The orientation course never told us why we were doing this, this way."

"It's too confusing at first."

"I'm not motivated."

"I wasn't prepared for how much I had to do on my own."

Technology Problems

"My computer wouldn't show the videos, so I missed a lot."

"I got bored waiting for everyone to get online."

"The technology doesn't work."

"I don't know what to do when it freezes up."

"I get tired reading that much on a computer screen."

"I couldn't jump from one screen to the next without waiting."

"The computers failed at times."

"You shouldn't make the students responsible for making the equipment work right."

On Support

"They never give me time to sit down and do it."

"I found no place where I wouldn't be interrupted."

"My boss doesn't believe I'm working."

"My boss lets me go to classes, but keeps interrupting me when I'm online."

"The help desk saved me. I'd never have completed the course if they weren't around to answer my questions when I first started."

"No one in my department has time to use it."

"It didn't take me away from the office."

"The online instructor needs to be accessible off-line."

"The instructor sometimes took a day to get back to you."

"e-Learning just isn't our priority."

In General

"I don't see that e-learning is any better than taking a class."

"At least I didn't have to buy a textbook."

"With e-learning you don't have to take notes."

"I don't see any advantage in it."

"It's boring!"

"It lets me learn what I need."

"It's fun at first, but it gets tedious quickly."

"It's no better than a book."

"I just don't like it!"

"You only get out of it what you put into it."

About the Editor

George Piskurich is an organizational learning and instructional design consultant specializing in e-learning design, performance improvement analysis and interventions, and telecommuting initiatives. With over twenty years of experience, he has been a classroom instructor, instructional designer, and corporate training director. He has developed classroom seminars, multi-media productions, and distance learning programs.

Piskurich has been a presenter at over thirty conferences and symposia, including the International Self-Directed Learning Symposium and the ISPI and ASTD international conferences. He has authored books on learning technology, self-directed learning, instructional design, and telecommuting, edited books on instructional technology, HPI, and e-learning, and written many journal articles and book chapters on various topics. He can be reached at (478) 405–8977, by email at Gpiskurich@CS.com, or through his website: GPiskurich.com.

Index